THE LOG CABIN BOOK

In the Wilderness.

THE
LOG
CABIN
BOOK

A Complete Builder's Guide to Small Homes and Shelters

OLIVER KEMP

Illustrations by the author

DOVER PUBLICATIONS, INC.
MINEOLA, NEW YORK

Bibliographical Note

This Dover edition, first published in 2016, is an unabridged republication of the second (1911) revised edition of the work, originally published by The Outing Publishing Company, New York, in 1908, under the title and subtitle *Wilderness Homes: A Book of the Log Cabin*. All of the original line illustrations have been reproduced here in black and white.

Library of Congress Cataloging-in-Publication Data

Names: Kemp, Oliver, 1887–1934, author, illustrator.
Title: The log cabin book : a complete builder's guide to small homes and shelters / Oliver Kemp.
Other titles: Wilderness homes
Description: Mineola, New York : Dover Publications, 2016. | "This Dover edition, first published in 2016, is an unabridged republication of the work originally published by The Outing Publishing Company, New York, in 1908, under the title and subtitle Wilderness Homes: A Book of the Log Cabin."
Identifiers: LCCN 2016023359| ISBN 9780486810782 (paperback) | ISBN 048681078X
Subjects: LCSH: Log cabins—Design and construction—Amateurs' manuals. | BISAC: CRAFTS & HOBBIES / Woodwork. | HOUSE & HOME / Design & Construction. | SPORTS & RECREATION / Outdoor Skills. | HOUSE & HOME / House Plans. | HOUSE & HOME / Woodworking.
Classification: LCC TH4840 .K46 2016 | DDC 694—dc23 LC record available at https://lccn.loc.gov/2016023359

Manufactured in the United States by LSC Communications
81078X02   2019
www.doverpublications.com

FOREWORD

IF you love the out-of-doors, this book was written for you, to crystallize and bring into reality that vague longing which you have felt for a lodge in the wilderness.

Somewhere the trail has led you to the ideal spot in the deep forest, by the shores of a smiling lake or within sound of the murmuring waters.

Wherever you may choose to dwell in the woods, there will be found abundant material for a log cabin, and a day's work will bring results big with pleasure and healthy enjoyment, for even the temporary sojourner in the wilderness cannot turn to better employment than that which will give him a home of his own handiwork.

FOREWORD

This you will own with a new sense of proprietorship that hitherto you have not known. Work of your hands, your pride in its possession will increase with the improvements suggested by its occupancy from year to year.

We have purposely avoided the elaborate log structures, which by courtesy are called camps, for they are beyond the ability of the amateur to construct, had he ever so much time at his command. When you desire something more than is here shown, consult an architect, and for the building of it, by all means "let" the job.

The designs which are given have all been built and allow of numberless alterations to suit the whims and requirements of the builder. This much you are sure of: from the first your cabin will have the charm of a home, it will nestle among the trees like a real companion of the forest, though nature must have a few seasons in which to " creep up to the doorsill and wipe away the scars of man's hasty building."

The methods of construction given are those of a thorough workman, though the operations may be greatly curtailed, especially in the smaller camps. A perusal of even the elaborate building directions will by no means daunt you. To have your home in the woods only two things are necessary, the time and the will.

In my own experience I have often wished for such a book as this, and I feel fortunate indeed in the friendship of Mr. D. L. Annis, of Sebec, Maine, to whose interested and practical tutoring I owe my knowledge of Log Cabin building.

Some years ago I contributed a couple of articles (which are incorporated in this book) on the subject to the magazine *Field and Stream*. The instant response indicated a need for the information contained herein. For that reason these pages

FOREWORD

were written during my leisure time in the woods and I send them out tried and tested.

Not the least important part of the book are the photographs, and in this connection I must acknowledge with pleasure my indebtedness for the valuable help afforded me by Mr. Harrie B. Coe, of Portland, Maine; Hon. Carter Harrison, of Chicago; Mr. George W. Kirkner, of New York; Mr. N. W. McNaughton, of Schoodic, and Mr. M. J. Marr, of Indian River, Maine, in supplying many of the photographs of their delightful Wilderness Homes.

x

CONTENTS

MAKING PLANS

CHAPTER I

PLANNING the woods home is a period of considerable pleasure. Everything about it will suggest the forest and the remote lake, where the big trout hide, and the deer come down in the evenings to feed on the tender grasses at the water's edge. It brings that great season near to which we look forward year after year from the city home.

The pleasure thus afforded is, however, but part of the satisfaction, for, guided by a sure knowledge of the possibilities and limitations of the subject, your plans will

3

save you an infinite amount of work and time when the building operations actually begin. Then if one is careful to erect it in a commanding position, and will take the necessary care to adjust it to the surroundings, the resulting harmony and utility will be a source of constant satisfaction.

In the matter of fitting the cabin to the site, you have a tremendous advantage over the builder of structures for other situations than the woods. So long as you stick to the one-story or story-and-a-half building you are safe, for the log cabin will belong to its place as surely as if it grew there. After all, are not the bowlders gathered on the ground where the future cabin is to stand and the logs felled in the encompassing forest? There is nothing new about it; chameleon-like, with a simple touch of stain on the roof, it will take on the color of its surroundings, particularly if you, as the builder, do not get in the

4

An Example of Cabin Much Too Elaborate for Amateur Building. Enough Trees have been Cut to Give All the Sunlight and Air Necessary, Yet in no Sense has the Forest been Pushed Away.

way. Let the material of the building show frankly for what it is. Let each part do its work honestly, and you need not fear for the attractiveness of your home. Its success will be measured not by its size nor by its architecture after all, but by its comfort.

Fortunately there will be an outlook from every room, and we can let the light and air in from every side. The living room, with its high ceiling, will be given the choice of views, and we will call this the front of the house. In order to get all the out-of-doors possible into the house, plan for windows that are long rather than high.

Consider them as frames for the view, and while many windows are desirable, yet you must not forget that furniture of a sort must come into the calculation. Many a room has been built with no space left for the bed. It is commonly said that a house

5

cannot have too many windows, but a great number of windows does not necessarily insure the greatest amount of light, nor the best ventilation. But then again, in the woods, you will be surprised how dark the surrounding trees will make your camp.

Casement windows lend themselves very well to our style of architecture, and whenever they are used, should invariably open out. However, it is almost impossible to make them wind and stormproof, and they are always clashing with the screens.

Whenever possible, bring the chimney into the center of the house, to insure a more even distribution of the heat, and also make possible the connection from adjoining rooms with stoves, should the occupancy of the camp in fall or spring make these desirable.

For a similar reason, arrange your kitchen so that it can be absolutely shut off

6

A Wide Piazza is a Source of Real Pleasure. An Ingenious Use of Driftwood is Shown in the Hangers for the Oars. Note the Outside Finish of the Windows.

from the rest of the camp when desired. On very warm days in the woods, when the gentle zephyrs play around the tree tops but forget to come lower down, you will get the point of this argument. Be sure to look up the regular sizes of windows and doors that are furnished the trade from the factories, so that you can make the proper allowances.

Keeping the building down to one story will make the labor of construction comparatively easy, and the care of the house will for the same reason be made much lighter. This will give you considerable space overhead for storage, or even sleeping rooms. However, plan to save your living room all the space clear to the roof. Such an air of largeness and comfort is to be gained thereby, with the only drawback of a difficulty of heating, though with even a moderate fireplace a room eighteen by twenty feet, with a twenty-foot peak, may

7

be kept thoroughly comfortable except in the bitterest cold of the northern winters.

The veranda will be the most-used part of the house during the summer season. It should, therefore, be made generous in its width—ten feet is not too wide—and as long as conditions will admit of. Thus all the family may occupy it at one time, and during the very hot days, when eating out-of-doors is a luxury, it will be turned into a dining room far more attractive than any you could plan.

On a wide veranda hammocks may be swung without their excluding large and comfortable chairs, and here, even on a rainy day, one will scarcely be forced indoors. But if so, the chances are that the chill dampness will make a fire desirable. You will not suffer a loss with the exchange.

Set the windows of the sleeping rooms about four feet from the floor. It is

An Illustration of How Well a Wilderness Home May be Made to Fit its Environment.

curious how much of an added sense of security and privacy this will give. For there are those who feel uncomfortable in sleeping for the first time on the ground floor.

Measure carefully every inch of the way in your plan, and consider well the utility of every space; thus you will not find yourself cramped for room, and, on the other hand, you may save yourself considerable expense of labor and money.

You are not an architect, so be modest, and do not strive for architectural effects. Confine yourself altogether to ascertaining how few rooms you can get along with, and how to get those rooms to fit into the given space, so that each one will be large enough to fill the requirements. That is all.

When .the plans are satisfactory, you will make out a list of things required and send your order for them at the earliest

possible moment. Two months before needed would not be too soon in the South, six weeks in the North and West. This is not figurative language. I know of what I am speaking. Your list will look like this:

Number of logs needed.
Number of windows and sizes. (Include if possible frames, finish, and casings.)
Number of doors and sizes. (Include if possible frames, and finish.)
Amount of lumber for roofing and first floor, also veranda. (This may be the cheapest grade of spruce, planed on one side.)
Amount of hard pine flooring, two and a half inches wide, planed both sides.
Number of shingles. (Extra 1, cedar.)
Hinges for various purposes.
Round-headed screws for window casings.
Screws for all the hardware.
Locks.
Window fasteners.
Wire nails. Lath for shingles. Tenpenny for roof and floor boards, etc. Finish for windows, doors, etc. Spikes for rafters, etc. Eightpenny floor for flooring.
Building paper.
Creosote stain.
Number of barrels of lime.
Iron supports for fireplace arch.
Sheet lead for chimney.
Sink and short lead pipe for drain.
Firebricks for lining chimney.

Plans for the smaller "Hunting Camp" will require much less material than above.

In this Cabin at Beaver Pond, Maine, is Incorporated a Chimney Built of Logs and Lined with Mortar.

A Variation in Construction that Lends an Interest to the Finish.

However, I should advise a careful study of your requirements even in this case, so that time may be saved when you have reached the ground and are ready for business.

The pitch of the roof is important, and particularly in regions of heavy snowfall. A fairly steep roof is therefore desirable, both to lessen the strain and to prevent the snow water from being backed up under the shingles when a thaw is followed by a freezing period.

Over the bedrooms and kitchen, etc., a floor of hard pine, planed on both sides, may be laid, and this will always give you considerable space in which to stow things, or, as mentioned elsewhere, may be turned into a sleeping room, with spaces between the floor and the roof on either side of the room partitioned off for storage.

Avoid hip roofs if possible, though occasionally, in a rather long stretch, they may

11

be used to lessen the monotony. Try to
keep the whole structure under one con-

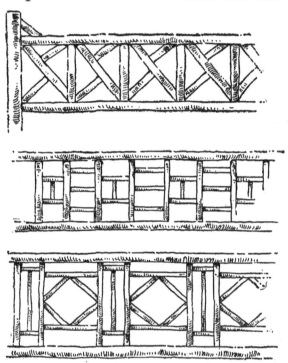

Suggestions for Rustic Railings, Etc.

tinuous roof, for the sake of economy of
time and money. The construction of a

12

If the Roof is Very Flat in Regions of Heavy Snowfall, the Supporting Beams Should be Well Braced and of Stout Timbers.

hip or a valley roof is not difficult, but they present features that require care in building that they may be water-tight and strong.

The matter of rustic effects in the porch railings, etc., is one allowing a wide latitude to your inventive faculties, and the entire outside of the camp may be given a special stamp of individuality by a proper handling. In regions where white birch may be obtained, one could ask for no finer decoration.

THE FIREPLACE

CHAPTER II

THE FIREPLACE

YOUR lodge in the wilderness demands a heart to make it lovable—the fireplace. And you will want a generous hearth built for service rather than for show, thus will the old ties with nature be renewed.

And do not fear that building for service will detract from its beauty. My word for it, neglect its architecture for its utility and it will still "look right," though here as elsewhere we want no sham honesty or fake simplicity. Build it for the purpose intended, and when the chill gray days do come it will warm your very soul with cheer and make the home complete.

A fireplace of stones, with its rough-hewn log shelf, falls at once into complete harmony with the cabin and its life. It needs no adornment, yet everything, from the flintlock gun to a snowshoe, seems a part of it.

Select your stones with a care for their coloration, and the moss and lichens clinging to them.

The opening should be three or four feet wide, or even five; if the room be very large, about two feet deep, and not over twenty-five or twenty-six inches high. To hold cordwood, the dimensions are about four feet six inches wide and three feet six inches high. A fireplace should not be too deep, or an important proportion of the reflected heat will be lost. The sides should not be set at right angles to the back, but should slant to nearly an angle of forty-five degrees.

Now, the draught of a fireplace is most important, and a mistake in the construc-

18

A Fireplace of Rare Charm and Interest.

tion is almost impossible to correct. Slope
the back of the fireplace inward toward the
front, terminating at the throat about four

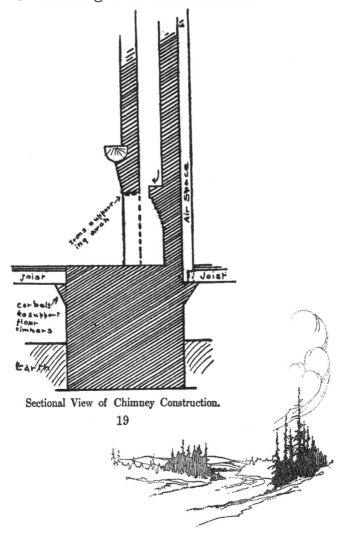

Sectional View of Chimney Construction.

19

or five inches above the front of the arch. It should be drawn in until the throat is narrowed down to almost three inches. This will leave a ledge which will accelerate the draught, and form a shelf to prevent too great a volume of air from rushing down the flue.

Have the flue large; it should not be less in area than ten per cent. of the area of the opening of the fireplace. Constructed in this way, you will have no trouble from a smoky fireplace.

Under no circumstances attempt to build the chimney with a woodwork support. Dig down in the earth and lay a solid bed of rocks and mortar as a foundation, the full size of the chimney and the hearth, which should be about twenty-four inches wide. This will keep the woodwork well away from the fire. Neglect of this point, where I rested my hearth on woodwork, came very near to having serious results.

This Fireplace and Chimney was Built by an Amateur and
Occupies One Side of a Log Studio.

Corbels may be built out to receive the ends of the floor joists.

The fireplace should be lined with fire-bricks, and iron bars must be put in to support the superincumbent brick or stone-work. Do not trust too much to your arch, if you have one. A couple of iron bars, about two inches wide and a quarter of an inch thick, will make all secure.

Mortar is not difficult to prepare. Get unslacked lime and put it into the box which you have made to hold it. The lime is now to be slacked by wetting with water. As you throw the water on it will heat up and steam, and enough water should be added from time to time to keep the lime from burning or slacking dry; it should be kept about the consistency of thick paint. Lime should be slacked for several days before the time for using it.

To a cask of lime add six bushels of sand, and stir until the lime and sand are thoroughly mixed. It should be thinned with water until it mixes easily with a hoe. It should stand for two or three days until ready for use.

Cement will greatly increase the strength of mortar, and, when desired, should be added in the proportion of one or two quarts of cement to each pailful of mortar. Remember that, with cement added, the mortar will set much more quickly than it would otherwise do.

Keep your work plumb by means of cords fastened by nails in the roof and floor. As your work emerges from the hole in the roof, select small and flat rocks and insert some sheets of lead, cut ten inches long by eight inches wide, in the different layers of stone in shingle fashion.

After the chimney is completed the shingles may be inserted in the layers of lead, and so make a tight joint around the chimney.

22

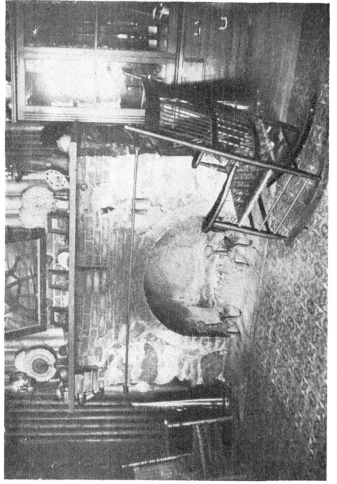

It is Possible to Combine Brick and Stone Into a Fireplace Full of Comfort and Cheer.

THE FIREPLACE

Now, if you are unfamiliar with the building of a fire, you will be vastly entertained by your inability to get the thing to burn. One after another the various members of the family will be inspired to try

Method of Leading Around Chimney.

their hands and lungs. For pure cussed contrariness, an open fire takes the honors. When you have all given up in despair and left in disgust, the thing is apt to start up of its own accord.

The shavings which have accumulated

23

during the building of the camp should be kept for this time. Between the fire dogs a generous supply of dry shavings; on top of them, a few short, thin pieces of larger wood; resting in the fire dogs, three sticks of wood with a space between each stick. Across these, three more sticks, and across these, two more. Light the shavings. When the fire is burning well a large greenwood log of maple or beech may be put against the back wall as a back log. On top of it another green stick should be laid and the fire drawn out to the front of the fireplace. A slight replenishing from time to time will keep a fine fire and the back logs will burn all day. At night the fire may be banked by covering the embers with ashes. In the morning this covering may be raked off, and fresh sticks laid directly on the glowing coals will soon spring into life again.

Soft wood will crack and sputter, and it

24

A Hearth with Many Cracks is Difficult to Keep Clean. The Standard of
the Table is a Piece of Driftwood.

If Rocks are at Hand to Build with, it is not a Great Task to Construct a
Chimney at Once Distinctive and Useful.

would be dangerous to leave a fire without some protection. Even the hard wood will at times throw burning coals out into the room. A fire screen is the solution, and is easily made of quarter-inch wire screen, fastened to a frame of quarter-inch steel wire. The screen should extend an inch all around outside the opening of the fireplace. It should not be flat, but should be from three to five inches deep. This will prevent sparks from flying out of the crack between the screen and chimney. The shape can be had by bending the screen over a box or similar form.

If a crane is contemplated, it should be put in place during the building of the fireplace. In the North, where beans are a prominent part of the bill of fare, it would be well to have a " bean hole " built in the center of the fireplace. Make it about twelve inches square, and provide a stout iron lid to cover it. An iron pot with an eccentric-clamped lid may be kept here. Pork and beans cannot be cooked better than in such an arrangement, with the hot coals covering it and left overnight.

26

THE AX AND THE TREE

CHAPTER III

THE AX AND THE TREE

THE one indispensable tool in the building of a log cabin is the ax. I know a man who, with no other implement, can erect a marvelously complete cabin; but this degree of efficiency we ordinary people may not hope to attain.

If you be wise, then, purchase the best ax possible. The cost of this will not be over $1.25. An inferior one may be had as low as 75 cents, but the steel is not there. Long before the camp is finished you will have discovered that an ax which bites in deep and holds its cutting edge is desirable. Axes come of varying weights, but for the average user one of three and a half or three and three-quarter pounds is about right.

29

Perhaps it has not occurred to you that the "handle" or helve was a thing to be considered, yet the dealer will put out an assortment which, if you examine them, will be found to consist of crooked and straight, thick and thin, and varying combinations of these. If you have never handled an ax, you will have some difficulty in deciding. Your only guide probably will be, after selecting one fairly crooked, to purchase the one which feels best in your hand. If your fingers are short, do not get a handle too large in diameter, and *vice versa*. Neglected, this point may occasion you a painful period of cramped fingers. I have seen men in the woods (and they forget to complain of any hurt) whose grip had to be loosened by the aid of the swinging hand. An extra helve should be taken always.

To "hang" your ax properly requires care, and is important. If it be hung too

30

far " out " or too far " in," or if it be out
of line, it will lessen very materially the
effectiveness of your stroke. Therefore,
slip the helve into place in the eye of the
ax, work the " bit " or cutting edge up
and down, to see whether it can be brought
to a proper position. This means that the

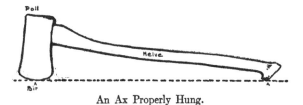

An Ax Properly Hung.

center of the bit and the knob on the handle
should touch if the ax were placed against
a straightedge, as shown in the plate.

If necessary to bring this about you will,
of course, cut off a little from the back of
the helve until the ax hangs properly. Be
very careful to see that the bit of the ax
comes in direct line with the helve.

About a half inch of the helve should

31

project through the ax on top. Now, with a chisel or another ax, split the helve straight across from the " bit " to the " poll," then select a piece of hardwood, of the width of the handle, and make a wedge, rather long and about three-sixteenths of an inch in thickness an inch and a half from the point. Turn the ax upside down and strike the end of the handle a few sharp blows. This will set the ax on tight. Sight it once more to make sure that it has not gone out of line. If all is right, insert the wedge in the slot and drive it in tight. Then with a saw cut off the projecting ends of the helve and wedge flush with the ax. You may depend upon it, this will never come loose. A small whetstone (one of carborundum is best) will keep the edge keen.

Occasionally, however, the ax must come to the grindstone, for in spite of every effort to avoid injury, the nicks will appear. Do not attempt to cut off the knotty stubs of hemlock—they are like iron. Batter them off with the poll of the ax.

It is best to fell your lumber in the spring, say from May to July. At this time the sap will run and the bark may then be easily stripped. After that, you may find some day that it is difficult or impossible to peel the bark; then the only alternative is to shave the bark off with a drawshave; but this spoils the beauty of the log.

To peel the bark from a tree or log, cut two circles completely around the log about four or five feet apart, and connect these with another cut lengthwise of the log. Insert the edge of the ax to start the bark. If the sap is running well, it will strip easily, requiring but little loosening from time to time with the ax or a " spud," which is a short stick of hard wood tapered at one end to a flat edge.

33

Should the bark be desired for roofing, it should be flattened out and kept away from the ground to dry.

Any of the soft woods may be used for building—pine, fir, spruce, etc.—according to the growth of timber handiest. Maple, birch, beech, etc., will be much too heavy to handle and hard to work.

It is a simple matter to estimate the height of a tree by standing off a short distance and guessing the probable height of the first branches. If they are ten feet from the ground, make mental divisions of the tree in ten-foot lengths, and you will be surprised how near your estimate will be correct.

Before you cut into a tree, make sure that it does not taper too suddenly, and sight it carefully that it may not have a bad crook in it that will make it unavailable. Certainty here will save you much labor, to say nothing of the regret which

34

must come to a lover of the woods with any wanton destruction. Keep in mind that *it takes only twenty minutes to cut down a tree, but thirty years' growth will scarcely replace it.*

Having decided upon your tree, make sure of the best direction for its fall. It is important that it should not lodge in the branches of neighboring trees. Should such an event come to pass, exercise every care in your effort to dislodge it. A falling tree has a way of trapping the unwary, the results of which are apt to be serious. Study the situation well.

Trim away very carefully all the underbrush within the reach of your swinging ax, and thus avoid injury. An ax diverted from its course strikes with the quickness of a flash.

Begin to cut on the side of the tree facing the direction of its intended fall. Your notch will be quite wide to prevent

35

the ax from wedging as it bites its way into the tree, a blow from above to make the chip and a blow from below to cut it out. Work slowly and deliberately, so that each blow may count, but do not exert yourself unduly. Let the weight of the ax do its share of the work. Eventually you will achieve some accuracy, and then the stumps will approximate that planed-off appearance which a lumberman leaves. Yours will not look that way.

When you have the notch a little more than halfway through the tree, begin a similar cut on the opposite side, somewhat higher than the first cut. In a thick growth you may have to cut very deeply, but presently the tree will pitch slightly in the direction of its fall, and at the next stroke it will crack and settle to the earth. Step to one side when this occurs, never in the opposite direction of its fall, for some trees have a nasty habit of springing back from the stump, and woe to the individual in their path!

For dressing small timber, cut two logs four feet long and about one foot in diameter. Bore three large holes through one of these logs, two about six inches from each end and one in the middle. Make three hardwood pins to fit the holes, and drive one through the middle hole so that it projects about one foot. Now fasten the pin upright by driving two more pins through the two end holes into the ground, to hold the log firmly. The other log should have a notch cut in the center about six inches deep.

Bore a hole through the log to be hewn, about four inches from the end, and fit it over the pin, the other end of the log lying in the notched stick. Snap a line for your cut, then you should commence with your ax to " score in and beat off " up nearly to the line. That is, strike a sharp blow with

37

the ax from the side of the log, slanting in toward the line, but not quite touching it. Another blow in the opposite direction will cause the chip to fly out. Arriving at the end of the log, begin hewing carefully to the line. You will be surprised how quickly all this can be accomplished. Of course, all the cutting is done on the side of the log. The work may be made more complete now by running a plane over it once or twice.

In the course of your work it may be your misfortune to break the ax helve, and you will thereby be confronted with the problem of removing the stub, which you wedged in with the idea of its never coming out. Horace Kephart, in his excellent book, " Camping and Woodcraft," gives a simple solution to the problem:

" When the stub of the old handle cannot be removed by ordinary means, it must be burned out. To do this without draw-

38

THE AX AND THE TREE

ing the temper of the steel might seem impracticable, but the thing is as simple as rolling off a log when you see it done. Pick out a spot where the earth is free from stones and pebbles, and drive the blade of the ax into the ground up to the eye. Then build a fire around the ax head— that is all."

A cant-dog and a cross-cut saw are tools which will greatly facilitate work on logs. Other tools which you will need on the better class of buildings are: Handsaws—rip- and crosscut, steel square, level, hammer, brace and bits, chisels, drawshave, two-foot rule, chalk line and chalk, bevel, compasses, large and small planes. Have your saws well sharpened and keep a good whetstone handy, so that your tools may never become dull.

Many of the operations connected with the building will take place in the spring, and in many sections this is the happiest

39

time of the year for the joyous mosquito, the black fly, the minge, the no-see-um and *ad infinitum*. Some protection from these pests is necessary, and a " dope " that can be smeared on liberally over face, neck, ears and hands should be provided. This is important, and overlooking so simple a thing may be the occasion for your quitting work after the first half-hour, with the necessity of going " to town " to repair the oversight.

There are several varieties of " dope " on the market, and about every woodsman has a kind of his own. They are all good so long as they will give a greasy coating, and this must be renewed from time to time. My own concoction is:

Oil of Pennyroyal.......................1 oz.
Sweet Oil..............................6 oz.
Ammonia...............................1 oz.

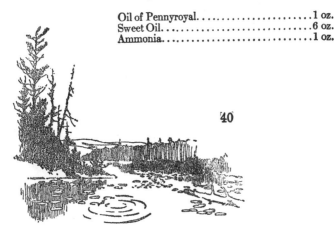

BUILDING THE CABIN

CHAPTER IV

BUILDING THE CABIN

CUT four stakes. Now, when you have decided upon the exact position you wish your building to occupy, drive one of the stakes at a corner. Measure the width of the building and drive another stake, and stretch a cord between the two. Then at a point as nearly as you can judge at right angles to this, measure off the length of the cabin and set the third stake. Now two more measurements of length and width from the first and last stakes set will give you the approximate position for the cabin.

Inside these stakes, and on the line laid down, you will build four temporary piers, either of stones or of logs, of about the height you desire the building above the ground, remembering that the floor will be six to eight inches higher.

Put your sills together on top of these supports, and begin to level them. For this purpose you will require a straight-edge about twenty feet long. Make it by nailing a couple of boards together that are about six inches wide, and long enough, of course, to give the desired length. Rest the straightedge upon the two parallel sills, and be very sure to place your level *on the center* of the straightedge, for this will sag some, and the sills may then be blocked up until they are level.

The sills are now to be set square. To do this, snap a chalkline down the center of two adjoining logs. From the corner measure six feet on one log and eight feet on the log at right angles. Then, with a ten-foot pole laid across to these points, push or pull the logs until the two ends of

An Expert at Log Cabin Building Can Make a Joint of the Logs
that is Almost Perfect.

the pole exactly touch the six- and eight-
foot points. Your building will be square,
and the sills should be spiked together.
Try the level once more.

Lay the foundation on a firm basis. You
will probably have to go below the loam
or upper crust of earth to the hard gravel
beneath. Secure flat rocks, if possible, and
if your piers (which should be every four
feet) are built of them, be absolutely sure
that each rock rests firmly and with no
" teetering " on those beneath. Break the
joints carefully. "If a rock doesn't fit,
turn it over," is an adage of the stonelayer.
It will usually be the solution.

Perhaps wooden posts would be better.
These will last much longer if their ends
rest upon a rock. But bear this in mind, a
rock in contact with the earth will sweat
and the moisture would in time rot the
posts. This is easily avoided by using *two*
rocks, one on top of the other. The upper

rock will never sweat. Cedar posts are best, though other soft woods, as pine, hemlock, etc., will do; the hard woods are not so durable. Treating posts to a good application of creosote will add much to their life.

When the supports are all fitted and in place they should be braced by two pieces running from the posts to the bottom of the sills. The temporary piers may be taken away when a sufficient number of the permanent piers are in place.

Divide the length of the cabin as nearly as possible into spaces of about eighteen inches and mark off these divisions on the long sills; this gives you the position of the floor timbers.

The sills should now be notched to receive them. The notches may be two or two-and-a-half inches deep, measuring from the top of the log, and about four inches across.

46

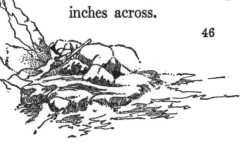

The floor logs must be squared on one side, and each end cut down to fit the size of the notches in the sills. Thus you will have an absolutely level floor, in spite of

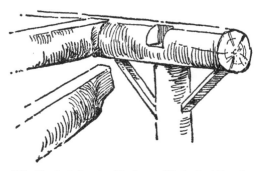

Sills Notched for the Timbers. Method of Bracing
Supporting Posts.

the fact that the logs used for timbers are of varying diameters.

Now you are ready to begin on the walls. Put your first log in place and mark it for the cut for the under log, leaving at least one foot or fifteen inches of the log to project at either end outside of the building. This can best be done with a pair of com-

47

passes, set the depth of the intended cut. Holding the compasses so that one point is directly over the other, let one point rest against the side of the bottom log, the other point touching the bottom of the top log. If you now move the compasses

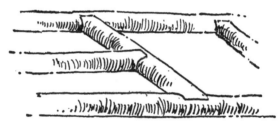

When an Opening in the Floor is Desired this is the Method of Handling the Timbers.

slowly over the bottom log, the upper point will mark the exact shape of the cut to be made. This should be done on two sides of the log. When the operation is completed, take the log down and turn it bottom side up to make the notch. The notch is always, of course, on the bottom to prevent the water from getting in and rotting

48

the log. The notch should be slightly scooped out in the center, so that the outer edges may be brought to a joint. The log is now put in place and, if it fits properly, may be fastened to the under log by a spike driven through the corner.

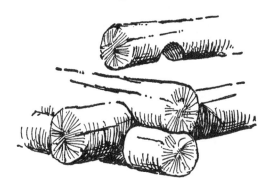

On a long reach on the sides of a larger building (eighteen feet or more) the logs should be fastened together by an additional iron pin, driven through about the center of the logs.

It will often happen that the poles are not straight; you may force the bend out

of the log by means of the cant-dog.
Therefore, if the upper log is to be pulled
in, set the hook in the upper log, with the
point resting on the lower one. Now
pull on the lever and the log will be forced
into place. Then drive your iron pin.

These iron pins may be had of any black-
smith, and consist of lengths of half-inch
rod, sharpened at one end.

If your logs are six inches at their larg-
est diameter, pins of ten inches in length
will be about right.

The logs should be laid alternating butts
and ends, and from time to time measurements should be made to ascertain whether
the four walls are going up of equal
heights. If not, look through your logs
and select those of larger or smaller diameters, so that the difficulty may be fairly
met.

When you reach the height of the windows and doors, make two saw cuts in the

Constructed in this Manner a Considerable Amount of Time and Labor is Saved by Doing Away with the Necessity of Notching the Logs at the Corners. The Windows are Made to Slide.

last log and almost through it. This leaves an opportunity for the further sawing when the time comes. It would be disastrous to make the openings now, for the corners of the building would be left entirely unsupported.

You will have found it no easy task to raise the heavy logs into position; as the walls rise, the difficulty increases. You will need skids on which to roll the logs up, and these are merely two logs laid from the ground to the top log. Lay the new log at the foot of these. On the upper log of the cabin fasten a rope opposite each skid. Carry the ropes down and around the ends of the log to be raised and back again to the top log. The log may now be easily drawn up by means of the ropes.

To make the corners without notching the logs cut two-inch planking to the height of walls, of about the width of diameter of logs to be used. This will make eight pieces which are to be put in place at the four corners of the camp,

51

resting on the sills, after the four logs for the first tier are squared across at both ends, cut to the exact length, and laid in place.

Spike the planks together to make V shaped posts and set them against the log ends, driving spikes through the planks into the logs, after they have been plumbed and temporarily braced. Proceed to log up the house. Then, as a finish, four logs are to be hewed on two sides to fit into the corner planks and spiked into position. Saw them to the proper height and bevel after the rafters are in place.

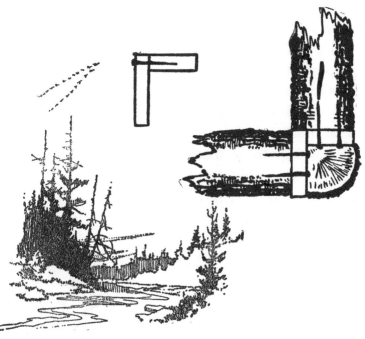

THE ROOF AND THE FLOOR

CHAPTER V

YOU should make a miter box now, so that the rafters may be all cut to a true and proper bevel for the ridge board.

Now build a staging down the center of the camp, high enough so that the rafters can be nailed easily. Then put the ridge board in place, after marking the positions for the rafters; this may be a board of the proper length of about seven-eighths or inch stuff, and slightly wider than the diameter of the beveled ends of the rafters.

The end logs may be continued to the peak, spiking them to the two rafters laid in place. With an ax, hew the ends of the logs down to the pitch.

Prepare the rafters with their bevel and put one temporarily in place while the place for the notch to fit over the top log is marked, leaving a proper length to project for the eaves. The rafter is then  taken down to cut the notch, after which it is once more put in place, where, if it is found to fit properly, two spikes are driven through the rafter into the top log and the upper end is made fast with three tenpenny wire nails.

When the last rafter is put in place it is time to cut your doors and windows. Snap a chalkline and nail a piece of inch stuff to the logs as a guide to the saw. A piece of two-by-six is spiked in place perpendicularly against the ends of the logs, and about two spikes should be driven in each log. You are ready for the roof.

56

THE ROOF AND THE FLOOR

Begin at the bottom to board up the roof, forcing the boards as close together as possible by driving a heavy chisel or other implement into the rafter close to the board, and pulling on the handle until the joint is tight.

Nail each board well at every rafter. When you have laid the boards nearly as far up as you can conveniently reach, fit in a board which do not nail. After nailing one board above this in place, remove the loose one and put it aside where it can be readily found when again needed. A mark will make certain of getting the right one in the right place. This open space left will afford a convenient foothold while laying the next series of boards, which proceed with as before. When the last board at the peak is laid then the open spaces may be fitted, as you come down, with the boards put aside for the purpose.

There will be a small space left between

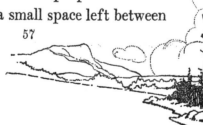

the top log and the roof, which should be filled in with a round stick, fitted between the rafters and spiked in place and the roof board nailed down to this.

Your shingles will be what are known as *extra 1.* They are a medium grade of cedar shingle, and the best for your purpose. Shingles may also be had in spruce, fir, or pine. These are cheaper grades and useful mainly for sidewalls, etc. They warp badly, split easily with the weather, and rot quickly. They are unfitted for roofing. One thousand shingles, laid five inches to the weather, will cover one hundred and thirty square feet 'of surface.

The life of a shingle may be very greatly prolonged if it be soaked in one of the many preparations of creosote stain on the market before laying. This, besides, will give your roof the tone which you have decided upon.

Staining the shingles after they are in

Note the Beveling of the Logs Around the Windows and Doors. Shows the Method of Setting in Rafters when Run Lengthwise of the Cabin.

place involves considerable hard work, and while the color is achieved no particular benefit of longevity is imparted to the shingle.

The creosote mixture may be put in a bucket or other vessel and the shingles dipped for about half of their length and thrown in a loose pile to dry.

For the sake of greater warmth, the lessening of draughts and the discouragement of insects, building paper should be tacked on the roof before laying the shingles. Paper strips should always lap over about three inches.

Commence to lay these at the eaves, leaving about two or two and a half inches to project. At the sides of the roof the shingles should project about half an inch.

After the first course is down another course of shingles is to be laid directly on top of them, remembering to break the joints fairly so that no joint comes within

an inch and a half or two inches of each other. Two shingle nails, driven six or seven inches from the lower edge of the shingle, will hold it firmly.

For the sake of facilitating the matter of laying shingles, nail two or three boards together that will be the length of your roof; these should be five inches wide. If you have been careful to get your first two courses of shingles on parallel with the eaves, this five-inch strip can now be put in place, its lower edge flush with the bottom of the shingles at the eaves. A few nails driven lightly through the five-inch strip at intervals will hold it in place. The next course of shingles may be quickly laid in place, breaking joints carefully as before. Now go back and nail them, then move the guide-board up for the next course, and so on to the top, sawing off the projecting ends of the shingles at the ridge. Leave a space of about eighteen

60

inches unshingled around the chimney hole until the leading is completed.

Of course, it is a simple matter to snap a chalk line on the shingles as a guide in laying succeeding courses, should you not desire to make the guide-board, but if the roof is of any size I would not advise the chalk method.

To complete the roof, a saddle board on the ridge is necessary, and this may be made of boards nailed together like a trough, after getting the proper bevel; a far better method, and more thoroughly in keeping with your log cabin, however, is to hew out a log for the saddle board. Do not fasten this in place, however, until the leading around the chimney (spoken of in the chapter on fireplaces) has been put in place.

The building may now be calked with cotton waste, moss, or excelsior, their relative value being in the order given. Cot-

61

ton waste, however, is by long odds the best, being cleaner, easier to use, and not given to swelling up and working out with the dampness and frost, as are the last two. A good calking tool may be made of any hard wood stick, shaping it somewhat like a cold chisel. It may be an inch or more in diameter, and the flat edge should be about two inches wide; with this and a mallet or hammer the waste may easily be driven firmly between the logs. With a crosscut saw trim off the projecting ends of the logs to about eight inches.

In the smaller camps it is sometimes desirable to have the rafters run the length of the cabin rather than from the eaves to the ridge. To accomplish this, the logs in the peak should be put in place, spiked, and cut to the pitch. Then the ridgepole is put in place and spiked, resting on the two opposite top logs. At intervals of about three feet down the pitch a notch is cut for the other rafters at the very end of the logs, making sure, as you lay them, that their outer edges are on a fair line with your pitch.

The roof boards in this instance are then cut to the proper length and laid across the rafters—of course, with the pitch of the roof.

While a single floor may answer the requirements, after a fashion, you should make your plans for a double floor, with at least one thickness of building paper in between; thus you are insured of warmth and dryness and freedom from mice and many strange and wandering insects. The second floor is not to be laid, however, until the masonry and other heavy work is completed; then lay your floor of "hard pine," and at once put whatever finish you may contemplate using on it.

Soft woods will not do at all for the floor. They soon show wear, and if any

63

care has been taken to make them attractive, they will quickly part with their early
promise, and no amount of work will make
them right again.

Hard pine or North Carolina pine
makes the best floor for the purpose, with
boards not over two and a half inches wide,
hammered up close and blind-nailed. This
may seem somewhat extravagant, but the
economy will become quickly apparent.

The smaller camps are sometimes left
unfloored, and while a camp built this way
may be kept quite clean, there are many
who object to bare ground. A good floor
may be made of poles with the upper surface squared. This flooring is perfectly
solid and good, but vermin of various sorts
will soon find the cosy home provided beneath the floor, unless the cracks are kept
well calked with moss, etc.

Do not permit yourself to be drawn into
considering thatched roofs, etc., and bark

64

The Saddle-board is of Peeled Logs Fitted in Position. Note the Tall Windows in the End which are Hinged and Also do Duty as Doors. The Porch is Supported by Slender Iron Rods. In very Cold Climates this is Desirable, as the Frost Cannot Get Sufficient Purchase on the Rods to Heave the Structure.

roofs are generally a delusion and a snare. If shingles are not available, used tarred paper. This is by no means long-lived, but is tight while it lasts, is easily put on and equally easy to renew when the occasion requires. For many reasons a camp in the wilderness has a tendency to attract and hold the dampness. Therefore, avoid the causes as far as possible. A leaky roof is an abomination.

Birch bark, of course, makes the best roof of all the barks, but it has a tendency to warp and crack that requires you to be very careful in laying it. Of course, it must be peeled in the spring, and should be " shingled " on the roof carefully, else you will find that the winter snows and ice have made a sad job of your work. The little camp shown on page 114 was roofed with birch bark some seven years ago, but my memory of its warmth and dryness was sadly shattered when I revisited it last summer for the purpose of making the photographs.

Should your plans call for a "hip" roof, the construction is the same as that

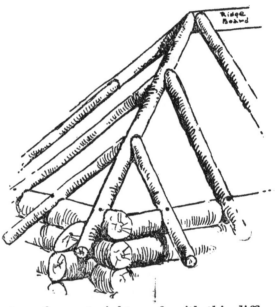

given for a straight roof, with this differ-ence: the ridgeboard ends at the point of the new slant, and two rafters are run up from the corners of the building, meeting

66

at the point in the roof. Then other rafters are fitted to these, ending at the eaves as before.

If you are wise you will purchase your windows with their finish, casings, etc., and thus have a tight and satisfactory job. They are easily set in place and the method of procedure will be at once apparent when you see them.

Steps to the porch may be constructed very simply. If you need three steps, determine the width of each tread, say ten inches. Cut two logs thirty inches long, about seven or eight inches in diameter, and face the top of the logs. Then cut two more logs the width of two steps combined, or twenty inches. After facing these, lay them on top of the first two logs, keeping the back ends of all the logs even. Now, two more logs of the width of one step, or ten inches, faced and laid as before, gives you a solid base on which to nail the treads.

Should your plans call for a sheet-iron pipe for a smokestack, care must be taken that the woodwork be kept well out of the way. Cut a circular hole in the roof at least six inches wider in diameter than the

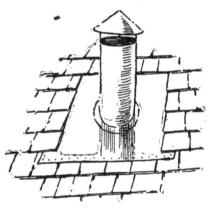

Safe Method of Bringing a Stovepipe through the Roof.

stovepipe. Have a large piece of galvanized tin with a tube three inches long set in it. This is to be fastened to the roof and then the shingles put down on it, keeping them well away from the smokestack. At the bottom the tin will lay on top of the

68

shingle course, while the upper edge will be pushed under the shingles.

In the hunting lodges it may not be practicable to " carry in " such an arrangement. A substitute may be made from a section of stovepipe, opened at the seam and flattened out. Mark with another section of pipe the size, and cut this out without attempting the turned-up part. When the sheet is fastened in place the pipe may be simply shoved through. This is not, of course, absolutely water-tight, but it will do.

69

THE CABIN AND ITS
ENVIRONMENT

CHAPTER VI

THE CABIN AND ITS ENVIRONMENT

THERE are two factors which must be considered when the time comes to fit the cabin to the situation. First, the fixed meteorological conditions, such as sunshine, the prevailing summer breezes, etc., and next the outlook. These may present conflicting claims. It is hard to generalize about unknown sites, but a few essentials must be kept in mind for any situation.

Give the prospect first place, for your wood home is to be regarded rather as a shelter into which you have brought all the great out-doors possible, and to which you may turn when the real out-doors shall

73

make you seek it. Sunlight you must have, for part of the day at least, especially during the early morning hours. It is universally conceded to be more hygienic the more the camp is exposed to the sunlight. For this reason, when the time for clearing away the trees comes, thin them out around the camp more than you have ever intended to do with a wood home. Thus the sunlight and aromatic odors of the forest will rush in upon you, and the cabin will take on an added charm.

Of course, you will not build in a marshy or low situation. In the woods it is well to look for indications of what occurs during or after a protracted period of rain. Otherwise you may build in a spot which seems ideal, only to find that your cabin is directly in the path of all the rushing surface water of your vicinity. Therefore, seek an elevation so as to have good drainage.

74

Detail of Steps and Rustic Work.

THE CABIN

Naturally one of the first considerations you will give to your future site will be that of the water supply and its purity, for much depends upon this.

If a spring be at hand it will more than repay considerable care on your part. Bank up the earth about it for a considerable distance to discourage surface water from working its way in, then dig down a short distance and wall the spring up with either stones or brick laid in Portland cement, the whole smoothed off as neatly as possible to facilitate the cleansing which must be done from time to time. A covering of some sort that will permit active ventilation should now be erected over the spring to keep out falling leaves and refuse. Care should be taken to keep all rubbish, etc., as far from the spring as possible. Slop water of any kind should never be thrown near the spring. To keep the earth clean in the vicinity of the water supply is of the greatest importance and requires constant watchfulness.

Should it chance that the spring is upon an elevation, it would be a simple matter to pipe it into the house, thus securing running water. The pipes may be laid on the surface of the ground and disconnected in the winter after having the water drained from them. It is not advisable to have drinking water stand. If it is necessary, however, to store it for a time, an earthenware crock or vessel is the proper thing. This should be well washed and scalded at frequent intervals.

Ponds and streams are not desirable sources of supply for drinking water because of the vast surface drainage they receive.

Should you be fortunate enough to have a small brook running near, by all means endeavor to dam it, and thus secure a miniature pond and waterfall. The banks of the pond may be made glorious with suitable plants, cardinal flowers, etc., and such an opportunity to build a curving rustic bridge is not to be neglected. Cover up your traces, however.

Now, an important feature of your wood home is proper sewage, and this demands attention. The outhouse should be built to accommodate, under the seat, a movable box lined with zinc or, better still, a galvanized iron pail, not too large, and made to fit close under the seat. This should be supplied with a layer of dry earth or wood ashes and the contents removed at frequent intervals, to be buried and covered with earth. Soil near the surface (if not too sandy) is in a large degree able to destroy organic matter; the waste should not, therefore, be buried deeply. One foot is quite sufficient.

Garbage is best disposed of by burning. If this is not possible, dig a hole for it and

cover it over with earth. A sprinkling of chloride of lime is recommended before covering. This will lessen materially the number of house-flies.

Look carefully after the overhanging branches of trees near the camp and trim the dead ones off to forestall any accidents to your roof or window glass.

Whenever a branch is removed, whether a dead or a live one, it must be cut off close to and even with the trunk, no matter how large the wound. The new wood and bark will then in time cover the denuded space. If the branch is not cut off close to the tree the projecting stub soon decays, the bark falls off and the rot penetrates quickly to the heart of the tree.

In removing a large branch, enough of the outer portion should be first sawed off to prevent its weight from splitting the wood downward. All wounds should be covered with white lead, coal tar, or creo-

Around this Cabin the Landscape Features have been Carefully Looked After, Though Nowhere is this Apparent. The Little Patch of Grass Gives a Homelike Touch that is Very Restful.

sote. No pruning should be done, however, until the fall, if possible.

Occasionally it may be necessary to remove a rock, and while this looks like a great task, if the rock is large, yet after all the matter is comparatively simple. Slaty rocks may be easily separated by starting a wedge in the different strata and with a few sharp blows an entire slab will loosen and may be disposed of.

Granite, etc., is a little more difficult, though if tools are lacking a hot fire may be built on and around the bowlder. This should be kept going for some time. Then cold water thrown on the rock will cause it to split and crack as though a charge of powder had been under it. A good blasting powder is perhaps the quickest and most efficient, and if you should decide to use this, get the brand known as Hercules, made by the du Pont Company, who will send you simple directions for its use.

79

This brings us to the question of what is best to be done with the landscape features about us. With some this means a general clearing up. All the rocks, bushes, etc., must go. But there are times when the big bowlders, which are never easy to remove, may be made most attractive. Virginia creeper or honeysuckle will twine lovingly about it if you give them a start, and doubtless the moss and lichens have already done their work in the beautifying. At its base the woody plants and ferns may be gathered. Ferns may be used to advantage in many places, and they will repay the care you take in setting them in the situations where you desire their mossy soft green effect. They are best transplanted in the spring or early summer. Some of the stronger growing may be moved at almost any time during the growing season. Care should be taken to secure a good-sized ball of earth with the roots,

80

and then in planting they should not be buried too deeply, and have the sod pressed firmly about the roots.

An occasional note of color may be had in the sunnier situations with either the creeping or dwarf nasturtiums.

Whatever is done, however, with plants, should in no sense suggest the city or country gardens.

Roadways into the camp are oftentimes desirable, but the building of a road through the forest is a question of men and teams. Lumbermen estimate that the cost is about one dollar a rod.

You will be surprised, however, how much one or two men can accomplish in a day in the matter of building paths or trails. Prospect over the ground carefully and decide upon the smoothest and most practical route, then with your ax blaze the trail. Now commence in the underbrush and small stuff. Some will

have to be cut. Cedar, etc., may be up-
rooted and dragged out with a little effort.
Throw the rocks and pieces of stumps into
the holes; knock the tops off the hummocks
into the low places. Whole sheets of earth
and moss may be stripped from the rocks
and used to fill in and cover with. Thus,
with comparatively little effort, a smooth
trail through the woods is made. Should
the trail take you over any sudden depres-
sion, build a rustic bridge. Two or three
logs laid side by side will make it, and
handrails may as easily be put in place. A
little rustic bridge or flight of stone steps
at some unlooked-for point gives a note
of pleasant surprise that is well worth
while.

Take extraordinary care that no fires
get started. In the forest it is a common
thing for a fire to work its way under-
ground without a sign, until suddenly it
will burst into a waving flame, terrible and

82

inexorable. Even when you have apparently stamped out the last spark and flooded the ground with water the fire may reappear in the next twenty-four hours, burning as determinedly as before.

If you have brush to burn, pile it upon the shore as far from the trees as possible, then wait for a favorable day. This will be immediately after a rain, either in a calm or with a slight breeze blowing toward the lake.

While there are innumerable advantages in living in the woods and also many delights, the mosquito is not to be classed among them. I am told there are two kinds, one with and one without " a sing." The latter is said to do the dastardly and deadly work, but all mosquitoes look alike to me. Where you are unaided in an effort to exterminate these pests you have almost as much hope of success as a fly on sticky paper. Yet if you will cruise around the camp for a few rods you will find many breeding places that might as well *not* exist. One day's work with these places convinced me that I could earn a considerable amount of peace for the season by carefully filling up every hole where water collected, even for a short period; in hollow stumps, depressions in the rocks, etc. When it was impossible to fill these up, a small quantity of crude oil was allowed to spread across the surface. A gallon will spread over acres in swamp land, and if the dose is repeated every three weeks it proves most discouraging to the mosquito. A neglected tin can with an inch of water in it will become the hatchery of some millions. Water is absolutely necessary to the hatching of mosquito eggs.

If you wish to induce the ducks to make longer stays with you, and to invite their friends also, plant wild rice in the shallow water along the shores of the coves or

84

This Cabin is Much Too Ambitious for Amateur Construction. It Shows an Interesting Use of the Rustic Details.

nearby stretches of still water. Perhaps
you have tried planting this in the past, at
no little expense and trouble, and have not
yet had the satisfaction of seeing the first
spear appear. The secret is this: the seeds
should never be allowed to dry. There are
places where this seed can be purchased
which has been kept in water from the
moment of gathering, and which will be
sent you packed in damp moss. This seed
will almost invariably grow. To any one
practically interested, who will write me, I
shall be glad to give the address.

Upon request, the United States De-
partment of Agriculture, through its Forestry Bureau, will send you pamphlets,
etc., that will be of the utmost importance
if you own more than an acre or two of
wooded land. Wood lots to which the
principles of forestry have never been ap-
plied very commonly offer a good chance
for " improvement cuttings." The pur-

pose of such cutting is to secure needed material, utilize timber which would otherwise go to waste, and make room for other trees to grow. In making improvement cuttings, look especially for two classes of trees in addition to those already indicated as desirable for removal. These are (1) over-mature trees which are beginning to decay and will rapidly lose their value, and (2) "suppressed" trees—that is, those whose crowns have been overtopped by their neighbors so that they can no longer compete for room. A few years of careful cutting in your lot will greatly increase the beauty of your stand of trees. Meantime you will be abundantly supplied with firewood.

An ice house is almost necessary where the camp is occupied during the warmer months, and where you are compelled to rely on a private supply of ice you will do well to erect a place for its storage.

THE CABIN

Ice may be readily kept in a structure of logs that has been thoroughly chinked or calked, digging down into the earth if you desire, though a building on the surface does quite as well, particularly in a woody position, where the trees give almost continual shade. The door should be made hollow and the space between filled with sawdust. Ten by twelve feet square and seven feet to the eaves would be about the right size. A floor should be made of poles set not too tightly together, to allow a free outlet for the melting ice. At the peak a small hole should be left for ventilation, and this should be covered with a screen to prevent insects, birds and vermin from getting inside.

A neighbor will fill this house with ice in a day, so that aside from the sawdust and the hauling of the same the cost is trifling and the advantage great.

In storing the ice the cakes should be

87

kept six or eight inches from the walls all around and the space between well packed with sawdust. Then, besides, the cakes should all be thoroughly packed on every side with sawdust to prevent their freezing together and also to assist in preserving them.

A boathouse is part of the equipment of the camp, and may be made an attractive feature, for with it may be combined dressing rooms for the bathers, to say nothing of an outlook from a balcony. The height of the water even on lakes is constantly changing, and this demands a float to make the landing of canoes or the embarking into launches easy. The raft idea may be employed, though it should be remembered that the float must be drawn out of the water during the winter, and logs are much too heavy to handle. Casks are the thing, and with a little ingenuity they may be framed in such a manner that the whole

88

float may be readily taken apart and drawn ashore.

Put a roller on the end of the float, so that canoes or rowboats may be drawn up on it with as little damage as possible, and it would not be amiss to pad a portion of the edge of the float with cushions of burlap or canvas stuffed with soft material, to act as fenders and save the paint and varnish. A gangway will lead from the float to the boathouse, and a small padded truck will facilitate the matter of getting the floating stock under cover away from the weather.

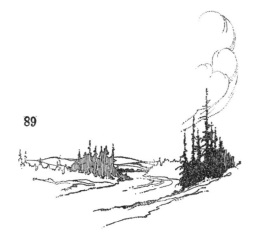

INSIDE THE CABIN

CHAPTER VII

YOUR first care with the interior is to take off the look of newness. There is a charm peculiarly its own about the walls of a log cabin, for even now, untouched as it is, you sense the spirit of the mountain and the lake which has been built into it with every log rolled into place.

The floor needs toning down with a stain (for paint is not permitted inside the cabin), and when you have decided upon what tone you want, do not be persuaded to buy some expensive concoction widely advertised as the best ever at three dollars a gallon. Make it yourself for fifty cents

or less and have exactly what you want.
A small quantity of oil paint thoroughly
mixed in a gallon of kerosene or turpentine
will fill the bill exactly. The intensity of
the stain is governed by the amount of
color used, and the color itself is modified,
if too glaring, by the addition of some
other color. Thus, raw umber will give a
fine brown tone, but if it is too red on trial,
add some black or blue or green. This you
will agree gives a wide latitude, but in
securing a brown or green tone for a room
it must be a "tone," and not a decided
color. I mention these two colors because
of their reminiscent feeling of the woods
they seem especially appropriate. Besides,
these soft tans and greens are always restful and pleasant to live with. Remember
that in a large use of a color it gains in
intensity.

After the floor is stained (make your
stain very thin) give it a coat of wood-

94

A Boathouse is Always a Necessary Adjunct to the Cabin. The Balcony
Idea is Naturally Associated.

An Interesting Stairway. The Treads are of Solid Norway Logs.

filler, and when this is dry finish either with varnish or wax.

The logs will of their own accord gradually assume a fine gray-brown tone, so that there is practically only the window and door trim requiring their share of the stain.

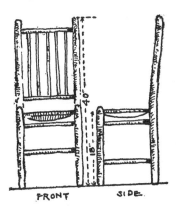

FRONT   SIDE.

Simple furniture to fit the situation is desired, and chairs and tables may be readily fashioned from the branches of trees. Care should be taken to select for this purpose such trees as have smooth bark that will cling. A spoke sizer will bring the

95

ends of the sticks down to fit the holes
which have been bored to receive them. All
the furniture should be put together with
glue and in addition a wire nail driven
through will keep the whole secure.

Seats and backs for the chairs may be

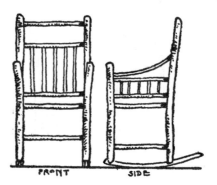

FRONT   SIDE

made of skins stretched across, or small
sticks may be nailed in place.

Window seats may be fashioned in much
the same manner, only now one may make
use of these for storage room, and the seat
should be hinged on, giving access to the
box beneath.

96

Window Seats are Always an Interesting Feature of an Interior, and in the Log Cabin they Make Excellent Receptacles in which to Store Things.

INSIDE THE CABIN

An excellent bed may be easily built, but be sure that you have taken the precaution to measure your spring frame. Springs may be done away with by using the old-fashioned method of " roping " the bed.

In the frame all around the bed bore half-inch holes six inches apart. Take rope of sufficient length and knot one end. Proceed to lace through the holes on opposite sides of the frame, pulling as tightly as possible, then make a temporary hitch. Go back to the first stretch of the rope and stand upon it, now to the next one in front, etc. You will soon take up the slack and the cords will be drawn tight. Fasten with a secure hitch. Now, from the foot to the head, stretch another rope as before, crossing the former work. This makes a good bed. Springs are better.

While the fit is on you there will be found many things to be made. A clock case, woodbox, pipe racks, gun and rod holders, clothes trees, etc., but in all these matters let utility rule. Do not try to overdo the " rustic " appearance of things. Keep them simple and take pride in building them of the fewest pieces possible.

Excellent draperies may be made of the dyed or plain burlaps and these may be made quite handsome with a simple design stencilled upon them. The only trouble to be met with in stenciling is in securing the design.

When this is had, secure a piece of rather

98

A Unique Closet for the Camp.   Note the Beveling of the Logs Around
the Door.

stiff heavy paper and cut out the design
with a sharp penknife. Resting the paper
on a small piece of glass will give a sharp
edge to the cut. When the stencil is cut
fasten it to the drapery in the position it is
to occupy. Have your oil colors ready
and also a quantity of gasoline or turpentine, for the color is put in more as a dye
than as a surface color. A little experi-
menting on waste pieces will give you the
proper consistency. Use a smallish brush
with stiff hairs. An artist's bristle brush
about three-fourths of an inch wide is just
the thing.

For curtains and thin stuff, as swiss,
scrim, etc., use a thin mixture of Diamond
Dyes. Unbleached muslin is excellent for
stenciling.

Take a small amount of the powder on
the end of a teaspoon, wet it with cold
water, then add one cup of boiling water
and boil for a few minutes.

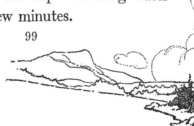

For crash, etc., use the aniline dyes (or tapestry dyes), but as they are rather dead use some of the Diamond Dyes in addition. Prepare them as above, adding color to get the desired shade.

Permit me just a word here with regard to the " pictures " for the wall. There are people who attempt to adorn their cabin with all manner of cheap lithographs, calendars, and other advertisements. In this day many of our finest out-door pictures are used by various firms for the exploitation of their wares, but in pity's name do not start a " collection " and use your rooms for the exhibition.

There are many portfolios of exquisite out-door pictures that may be purchased reasonably.

With but little work frames may be made for them of pine, which may be stained to accord perfectly with the view. A few of these may be hung, but don't

overdo the matter; treat it as if it were your city home in this regard. The logs of the walls are too fine in themselves and hold so much of what we seek in the open that we should try not to hide their charm. There is absolutely no room for the miscellaneous collection of posters, pine cones, college pennants, photographs, post cards, cotillion favors, etc.

Paddles and snowshoes lend themselves easily to the decoration of the rooms, and the introduction of a game head or two, or the mounted big fish that didn't get away, together with fur rugs for the floor, give the last note of the woodsy flavor.

Everything else must be rigorously excluded; thus the " atmosphere " will be preserved genuinely, and the suggestion of a museum never appear.

After the logs have had a seasoning period (and not before) the calked spaces may be plastered with white lime. If this

seems too glaring when dry, it will take a stain as readily as wood.

Not the least in importance of all the rooms is the kitchen, and considerable time and thought should be given it to secure the best possible results. In your plans you have arranged large windows that will give all the light and air possible. The problem of cleanliness is, however, somewhat difficult of solution in the Log Cabin —there are so many cracks and crevices to attract dust and vermin. In this room it would be best to plaster the cracks with lime mortar, then all the woodwork except the logs, including the shelves, should be given a good application of enameled white paint which may be easily wiped off with a damp cloth and thus be kept clean.

Have the kitchen sink broad and of generous size, with a shelf built at one end slanting toward the sink, so that the water from the dishes may drain that way. A

102

Suggestions for Stencils to be Used as Border Decorations.

plain cast iron sink will do very well and may be put in place by building a frame of the seven-eighths stuff at hand, remembering that the outlet end should be slightly lower, to prevent the water standing in the sink. The sink should be treated from time to time with a wash of hot water and soda or ammonia to keep it clean from deposits of grease.

103

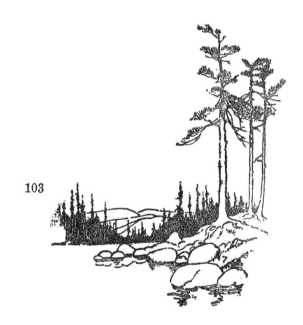

WHAT IT WILL COST

CHAPTER VIII

WHAT IT WILL COST

THE item of expense in the construction of a log cabin is usually difficult to figure, because ordinarily the price of logs is hard to determine without considerable correspondence.

I am therefore giving the probable cost of the cabin " Crow's Nest," and from this the approximate cost of similar structures may be determined.

The cost of the one-room or hunting cabin holds no relation to this, for the reason that nearly all the materials may be found on the spot, and as this class of cabin is usually put up in the more remote regions, the expense for " stumpage " may be very small or nothing. In this case you

will figure only on whatever material you
may decide to pack in and the cost of its
transportation.

A log cabin of the larger type is more
expensive to build than the regulation
frame " cottage." It has tremendous advantages over the frame structure, however, and at the same time retains every
point of excellence. The frame structure, nevertheless, can be erected much
more quickly.

92 logs for sidewalls and partitions	at	$.50	$46.00
20 logs for floor timbers	"	.50	10.00
7 logs for floor timbers, second story	"	.50	3.50
40 small poles for rafters	"	.10	4.00
20 small poles for porch rafters	"	.10	2.00
900 feet ¾ in. spruce boards, flooring	"	15.00 M	13.50
1,300 feet ⅞ in. spruce boards, roofing, etc.	"	15.00 M	19.50
800 feet hard pine flooring, planed both sides	"	50.00 M	40.00
100 feet 2x4 hemlock studding	"	13.00 M	1.30
3 yellow pine doors	"	.90	2.70
1 glazed yellow pine front door			4.50
12 windows	"	1.00	12.00
2 screen doors	"	1.00	2.00
10,000 shingles	"	2.10 M	21.00
10 bbls. lime	"	1.20	12.00
75 fire bricks	"	30.00 M	2.25
100 lbs. fire clay	"	01½	1.50
2 iron rods for fireplace arch			1.00
Hardware			3.50
Zinc for chimney			.50

WHAT IT WILL COST

Nails..............................	$2.50
10 gals. creosote shingle stain...........	5.00
Paint for window casings, etc., three coats.	2.50
Stain for floors, etc....................	1.00
Screening for windows.................	1.50
Total............................	$215.25

The cost of transportation will be largely governed according to the accessibility of the camp. There also comes into the calculation the chance laborer whose assistance may from time to time be required, and his daily wages in most sections are one dollar and a half.

SOME HUNTING CABINS

CHAPTER IX

SOME HUNTING CABINS

WHEN you have found the place where the shooting and fishing conditions are to your liking, a permanent camp is the thing, and circumstances often render advisable the building of a shelter more substantial and comfortable than the fragile tents usually carried upon outing trips. Moreover, an ax, a saw and a few pounds of nails are more convenient for transportation than the tent itself, and abundant material for a log cabin can be found convenient to any desirable camp spot in the woods. A log structure, no matter how modest, will always be more comfortable than a tent, and in cold weather there is no comparison whatever.

There are, however, campers and campers, and for a certain class the tent will be found advisable, for the reason that they will not be compelled twice to camp in the same spot.

Some go into the woods with a sublime indifference to dirt and litter of any kind. The floor of the cabin is never swept, particles of food lie all about, cobwebs everywhere, stove greasy, cooking utensils— *faugh!* There isn't a towel about the place. The soap is covered with bark dust and straws, and there is no arrangement for light at night. There are one or two contrivances like sawbucks to sit on, and the bed is made of boughs an inch thick, the stubby ends of which punch into you without mercy. There are no pillows provided; you must fold up your coat or stuff your bootleg and sleep as best you may.

114

After a Number of Years' Use the Stove Rusted and Burned Out, and it was then Added to the Outside Fireplace.

There are Many Days, Even in the Autumn, when an Outside Fire is Desirable.

SOME HUNTING CABINS

Outside the camp the same conditions prevail. Fish heads and bones, deer's feet and pieces of hide, tin cans and a slimy, odoriferous place by the door where all the dishwater is thrown. With all my love for the out-door life and the wildwood, I prefer my city studio.

These conditions are not all brought about by the owners of wood camps, for in the nature of things others will find them out and, according to the unwritten rule, occupy them. Unfortunately not all who accept the hospitality of your camp may be gentlemen, and it is to the rowdy class that we are largely indebted for the conditions above mentioned.

The failing seems to be universal. While hunting in the Rocky Mountains I came across a cabin, erected possibly two years previously, which was practically wrecked because some one was too lazy to cut the firewood which could have been gathered within two rods of the camp. They chopped up the floor and bunks and table instead.

Once during a severe storm up in the Hudson Bay country we were forced to give up our hunt for caribou and my guide started for a trapper's cabin which he knew to be nearby. The storm continued for two days, and you may imagine that our regards for the individuals who had occupied the camp before us were outspoken when we found that every cooking utensil had been stuck up in a conspicuous place and used as a target. They were so riddled with bullet holes as to make them useless.

But for pure cussed vandalism let me point you to the individuals from Ohio who, under the guise of being sportsmen, struck the Maine woods north of Sebec Lake and proceeded to take them apart. I will pass over their methods of hunting,

116

Front View of Squirrel Inn. With Just a Little Added Labor Any of the Hunting Cabins May be Made Distinctive and of Greater Comfort by the Addition of a Shelter Roof.

which, needless to say, was a highly successful slaughter, or their methods of fishing, which were equally effective. A friend and I had built a cosy cabin on a hillside, overlooking a gem of lakes in which the trout could always be found. One month afterward we went back to spend a few days, but the Ohioans had been there in the interval. They needed a raft, so they tore down the logs from the camp, and with some of the floor boards and the door managed to fashion a fine floating platform from which to fish! What would you say?

Now, an open camp has many objectionable features. It is cold, and to keep it warm requires an extraordinary amount of firewood. During a storm the wind may haul down an unexpected draw and pile the snow in upon you. In warmer weather they are fairly comfortable, but the mosquitoes just dote upon that kind of camp. True, a good smoke may keep them away, if you have luck and the wind is right. But my experience is that a mosquito enjoying moderate health can stand just as much smoke as I can. Then, of course, there comes the time in the midst of the best sleep ever enjoyed when the smoke apparatus goes out of business, and there is no longer any joy in life.

" Squirrel Inn " is a little camp that has given shelter to many sportsmen. Its floor dimensions are eight by ten feet. The peak is nine feet from the floor and the rear wall five feet. This cabin was built with no other tools than an ax and a saw. The great objection which I found with it was the lack of light, due to the use of windows that were too small. The roof was of birch bark, but this quickly became dilapidated and leaky. The floor was made of poles flattened on the upper surface and with the inequalities of the sides smoothed

Squirrel Inn is a Hunter's Cabin.

down. Two bunks, one above the other, occupied one end of the camp. To make these, stout poles were set across the cabin

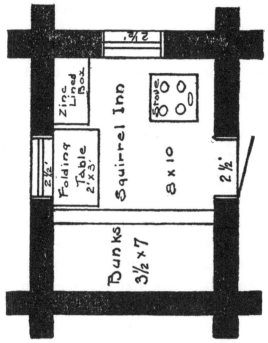

from wall to wall and on them burlap was stretched. Balsam twigs were then shingled on top of this. The box seat in the corner was lined with tin, and here matches, flour, candles, etc., were kept. A small stove occupied the remaining corner and the cooking utensils were hung on the walls behind it. The roof extending over the front made an excellent shade from sun or rain when it was desired to eat out of doors. A folding table occupied the rear wall between the box seat and bunks.

"Mouse Tower" is a type of the general run of hunting cabins, and the directions for its building will apply to any of the others. The completed cabin is eleven by seventeen feet on the floor. Nine feet at the peak and five feet at the eaves gives you the height and slope of the roof, which extends some four feet over the front of the camp. The first course of logs is laid directly on the ground and then leveled by knocking away the high places with the poll of the ax and building up the low ones with rocks well bedded. You have

120

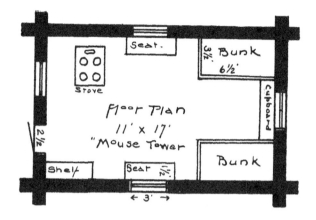

Floor Plan
11' x 17'
"Mouse Tower

Mouse Tower. The Usual Type of Hunter's Cabin Does Not Always Make Provision for the Storage of Dry Firewood, which was the Chief Design of this Four Foot Projection.

brought the window sash all set up, so there now remains only the door to build. This should have been figured on beforehand, so that it might be brought into the woods all cut to size, ready to nail together. The handle and catch may be made as shown in the drawing. Don't build a fireplace; have a stove and be comfortable. It doesn't look as well, but for the practical purposes of heating and cooking it is the thing. Set this as shown in the plan, leaving sufficient space for firewood between it and the cabin walls.

Don't build your bunks one above the other unless circumstances require it. Let the mosquitoes have a chance to get away from you if they want to; besides, fresh air is very desirable. The bunks shown will accommodate four ordinary men comfortably, and should be built about eighteen inches above the floor, with a guard board around the top about four inches high.

121

If you are in a region where balsam boughs may be obtained, cut a sufficient quantity of the little ends, which are about five inches long, and proceed to make your bed by shingling them in place at a slight angle, with the sharp or stick end down. This is a long operation, but once done it will last a long time and be fairly comfortable. The aroma of the pine, however, will be its chiefest charm, for no matter where one goes camping he carries with him the lingering memory of spring beds and mattresses, and their comfort is real and tangible.

The shelf near the door is convenient when cooking and during the inevitable dish-washing operation. The utility of the folding seats will be recognized by every one, particularly the practical joker.

Gun rack, coat hooks, etc., may be made of crotched sticks cut and fastened to the wall as shown.

122

SOME HUNTING CABINS

In the warm weather the heat of the stove is intolerable, so that a fireplace should be constructed in front of the cabin

on which to do the cooking. Make it of stones, built up as shown in the illustration, and place over it a pole quite high, from which wires can be hung on which to suspend the kettles.

Outside the cabin set two posts in the ground about eight feet apart, leaving about eighteen inches project. Cut a sap-

ling of sufficient length and fasten securely to the two logs, and you have a fine foot-rest in the summer evenings after the day's fishing, when the campfire is lighted and the stories and pipes are going.

You will find that several yards of mosquito netting will not be amiss when properly distributed over the door and windows, and if you will take a couple of hours for cleaning house on entering camp for the season you will be more than repaid by the absence of insects and spiders.

When the fall months come, with a mantle of snow flung wide over the landscape and the hunting season for big game is on, you will find it very convenient, after a day in the forest, to have a goodly supply of firewood on hand. So, if you are wise, you will have some cut and stored under the protecting eaves of the front of the cabin before leaving in the summer.

Hang a board in a conspicuous place, or

124

SOME HUNTING CABINS

bring a sign with you to tack on the door
which will read:

WELCOME

TO ANY BROTHER SPORTSMAN

PLEASE LEAVE THE CAMP IN AS
GOOD CONDITION AS YOU FIND IT

AND

PUT OUT THE FIRE

Thus the ethics of the woods may be
taught to the ignorant, and the thoughtless
be reminded.

In arranging the interior of these cabins
one thing above all else should be looked
after, the comfort of the occupants. With
Nessmuk, "I go into the woods, not to
rough it, but to smooth it." That, my
friend, is what you, too, must do if any
benefit to health or peace to soul is to be
derived from your recreation.

Now, in the hunter's cabin there is every

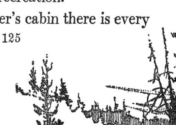

opportunity for being comfortable. This
means that some furniture should be made;
but not so much that there will be no room

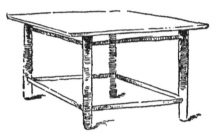

for the would-be occupants. Draperies
seem out of place in a camp of this kind,
but a substitute can be found in the various
animal skins procurable.

There are a number of fine sporting pictures to be had which can be framed with
ordinary white pine strips four or five

inches wide, on which birch bark has been glued. These, properly hung on the wall, will do much toward enlivening and beautifying the interior.

As cushions for the window seats, make sacks of some stout material—burlap is

good—and fill them with dry moss or balsam twigs and then cover the whole with skins.

Tables and chairs are easily constructed, as shown in the drawings.

Dispose of your guns, rods and paddles in such places as will have the best decorative effect, and after putting up a bookshelf (old magazines are absolutely new

127

on rainy days) add whatever seems necessary in the way of pipe racks, tobacco boxes, etc. Make a towel rack and provide a place for the soap. Then fill some large sacks of heavy muslin or denim with very dry moss and soft evergreen twigs for pillows. Devote some space to a good map of your locality, properly mounted on cardboard so that it may not be easily torn. A kerosene lamp is an abomination. The wick is soon used up, the chimney easily broken, the thing reeks of oil and is altogether a source of too much attention. Candles are much better, though slightly more bulky.

If you are in a big game country, arrange a beam nearby the camp on which to suspend such game as may be brought in. If you have ever tried to raise a good-sized buck into place you may remember that it involved something of an effort. A big blacktail is harder to arrange, a caribou

128

If there are no Mosquitoes, Rain, or Snow, an Open Camp is a Fine Thing.

almost impossible, and a moose is the limit. The solution is easy. On one of your trips pack in some small blocks and tackle, and be sure to have your beam strongly braced and secure. Fashion a number of gambrels or sticks for spreading the carcasses. These are merely hardwood sticks eighteen inches or longer. Larger ones should be made for lifting the animals. Have a place for these where they may be found when wanted.

The door will need a fastening and, as it will swing inward, the fastening will of course be on the inside. A simple contrivance is shown in the drawing, which will serve better than any words to describe exactly what is required. Make the latch of hard wood, and if no other means are at hand to bore the hole on which it swings, burn it through with some convenient piece of iron. Attach a cord or thong to the latch, let it pass up above the latch for a

foot or so and then through a hole in the
door, whence it can hang down ready for
use. A small stick tied to the end will pre-

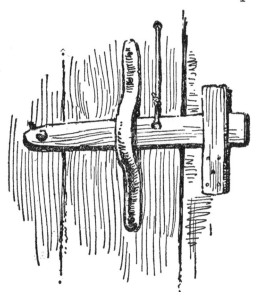

vent the latchstring from inadvertently
getting pulled inside the cabin.

Dig a hole into which the litter from the
camp may be thrown and covered with a
thin layer of earth. This will aid materially

130

in keeping down the number of house-flies.

The earth should be banked about the camp to keep the water from running underneath, and to shut out the draughts during the colder seasons.

131

A FEW PLANS

CHAPTER X

Wildwood

WILDWOOD is a thoroughly comfortable camp, easily constructed. The living room is large enough to contain a fireplace and chimney of ample dimensions. A thimble should be put in the chimney to accommodate the pipe from a stove in the dining room in the event of very severe weather, though the stove in the kitchen will keep the dining room very comfortable late in November in Maine.

The doorway between the living room and dining room might be made wider than is shown on the plan, with a simple drapery hung.

135

The stairway is two feet wide, with a rustic balustrade made of peeled poles about three inches in diameter. Underneath, in the dining room, is a low closet. The stairs wind half way up and cut through the partition, making a large closet underneath in the bedroom.

Upstairs there is quite a large room over the dining room and bedroom, ten by fourteen feet, with the space on either side of the room, where the eaves slope to the floor, partitioned off with a series of frame doors, covered behind with burlap, and hinged at the top to swing up against the roof. These are about four feet high, and so a very considerable storage space is obtained behind them. The room is used as a sleeping room, and contains one window.

In the kitchen everything is at hand. The stovepipe is run through the side of the house and is kept from contact with the woodwork by passing through a terra cotta

136

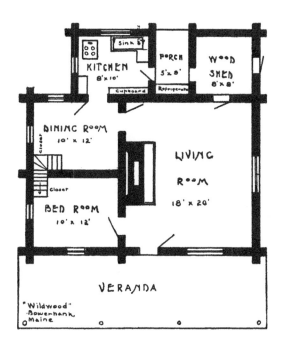

KITCHEN
8' x 10'

Sink 5'

PORCH
5' x 9'

WOOD
SHED
8' x 8'

Cupboard

Refrigerator

DINING ROOM
10' x 12'

closet

Closet

LIVING
ROOM
18' x 20'

BED ROOM
10' x 12'

VERANDA

"Wildwood"
Bowerbank,
Maine

"Wildwood" Nestles Cosily Among the Pines.

pipe of larger dimensions. The window is hinged at the top and opens inside against the roof.

The refrigerator is on the back porch, and over it are built a set of shelves with screen doors, where fish and game may be safely kept. The whole entrance to the porch is screened and a screen door is set in the center. The woodshed is convenient and contains one window with a door instead of a sash, through which the wood may be thrown for piling. Should the door leading from the woodshed into the living room be found undesirable, cut only a small one near the floor, which may be covered with a box seat. Thus you will acquire a wood box that may be readily filled from the woodshed.

Crow's Nest

Light and air are liberally provided for in the cabin design of Crow's Nest by very long windows opening on hinges. Their shape is also designed so that the view from inside the rooms is always properly framed. A window in the peak of the cabin should be small and capable of being opened by a cord from inside. This will afford a needed outlet for heated air during the long summer days. Provide suitable shutters to fasten over the windows on closing the camp for the season.

It will be found advisable in the smaller type of cabin to make the window seats in box form, with removable top for storage space. If but a single floor is laid, line the boxes with tin. This will protect your blankets, etc., from the mice and other vermin that are sure to get in the house.

If your spring is not nearby, a great labor-saving device can be arranged as follows: Take a barrel and fasten it at the right height, so that the water will run out of it by means of a small pipe, connecting

138

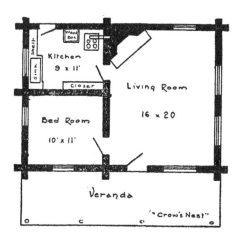

Kitchen
9 x 11'

Wood
Box

Shelf

Sink

Closer

Living Room

16 x 20

Bed Room

10' x 11'

Veranda

"Crow's Nest"

"Crow's Nest"

the sink and regulated by a faucet. A V-shaped trough, suspended under the eaves, will keep the barrel supplied nearly all the time. At any rate a half hour spent in filling the barrel now and then is much easier than carrying water each day. Of course, for cooking and drinking the usual trip to the spring must be made, unless one has the ingenuity to make the spring come to him. An icebox, built into the wall and capable of being filled from the outside, will be found a great convenience.

Don't forget to cover the adjacent wall with zinc before setting up the stove.

A Club House

A log-cabin structure is particularly adapted for the home of a club of out-door lovers. It was a great pleasure to design the club house shown here, in response to the following: " Please publish an article on how to erect a small, modest-priced club

140

house for a club of ten or twenty; we have
such a club, and we want to build one next
fall. Of course, a good-sized living or
club room would have to be incorporated
in the plan."

The simplest form of club house I can
think of is the camp of a logging crew,
which might be thirty-five feet long by
twenty wide. On one side are double tiers
of bunks, on the other side is the long table,
while the big stove occupies the center, and
around it the crew congregate after the
day's chopping to do their mending and
have a smoke before turning in. In about
twenty minutes the air is redolent of tobacco smoke, the smell of cooking and the
steam from the wet clothing hung about to
dry.

Now, if the objectionable features of the
logging camp could be eliminated and desirable ones substituted without any great
increase in cost, our task would be easy.

141

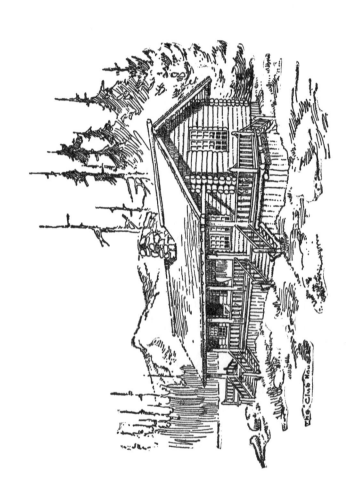

The Club House

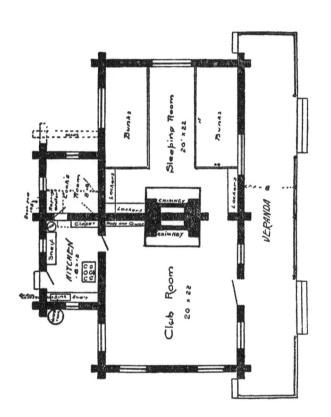

Unfortunately this cannot be done alto-gether; but the design shown combines all the good features compatible with a mod-erate-priced structure.

The club room is divided from the sleep-ing room by a partition of logs. In the center of the partition the chimney is set with opening for a fire in each room. The design of this should differ in each room to add the charm of variety. To the right of the chimney a doorway, hung with cur-tains, leads into the sleeping room, and to the left a case with spaces for guns and rods is provided. A swinging door leads into the kitchen.

In the sleeping room are tiers of lockers, which afford storage for the members' clothing, etc. A hole, covered with wire screening, should be cut near the top of each locker for ventilation. It is a good rule to incorporate in the " House Laws " that no damp clothing is to be put in the

144

lockers. Rig a clothesline back of the
house, where things can be dried and
sunned, and keep the sleeping apartment
as sweet and wholesome as possible.

The bunks provide sleeping space for
ten people, allowing three feet to each per-
son. If there are more than ten, a second
tier should be built, but should be at least
six feet above. The bottom of these bunks
should be lined with building paper, to
prevent the dust, etc., from sifting down
on the sleepers beneath. Build your bunks
very solid, with supporting posts every
three feet in front, and on every other one
nail cleats for ladders to the upper berths.

If two tiers of berths are used, the windows on either side of the cabin will have
to be omitted and the window in the end
made larger and very tall.

Under the shelves and closet in the
kitchen additional shelves should be made,
with doors enclosing your supplies. A

145

large hogshead for water should be set up outside, with pipe and faucet to the sink.

A door leads from the kitchen into the cook's room; but if the slight additional expense is no objection, three feet can be added to the length of the room and a partition put up. This will give a space for a refrigerator or icebox and ample room for storing supplies. Incidentally it would make a capital dark room in addition. A window should be put in the end of the pantry and a door cut into the refrigerator, so that the ice may be put in from the outside.

The Block House

The Block House is our concession to a two-story structure. Occasionally a site will be chosen for which this form of cabin is adapted, and it should be erected as simply as the drawing indicates. Any deviation in the way of elaboration would cause

146

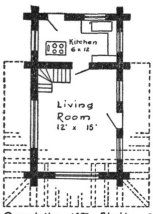

Kitchen
6 x 12

Living
Room
12' x 15'

Ground floor of "The Blockhouse"

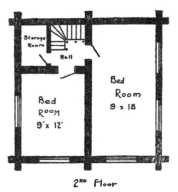

Storage
Room

Hall

Bed
Room
9 x 18

Bed
Room
9 x 12'

2ND Floor

"The Blockhouse"

the building to instantly lose character. However, a porch without any railing, if kept close to the ground, might be added to extend around three sides.

The living room is well lighted from three sides and the kitchen is practically separate from the rest of the house. A flight of winding steps leads to the upper floor, which may be partitioned off as shown, to make a large closet and a hall leading to two bedrooms.

After the last course of logs on the first floor is laid, the long timbers for the second floor are put in place, as indicated by the dotted lines in the drawing. At the front of the house shorter timbers are laid at right angles, their notched ends fitting *underneath* the last joist and resting on top of the course log of the lower story. The spaces left between the course log and the floor will be fitted with short logs spiked fast before laying the floor.

148

A FEW PLANS

Idlewild

For an easily constructed cabin, full of character and thoroughly homelike, Idlewild is ideal. There is always a shady nook on the veranda to be enjoyed, and the absence of a covering for this on either side permits an abundance of light and air to reach the living room.

This is a small cabin, but if it be raised three or four feet from the ground and the veranda railing and other rustic features are accented, the whole will take on an air of largeness and comfort, and the result will be thoroughly artistic.

Over the bedrooms and kitchen a floor should be laid, if possible, and a small window cut, in either of the storage rooms thus obtained, for ventilation. This space will make a vast difference in the temperature of the rooms beneath during a heated term.

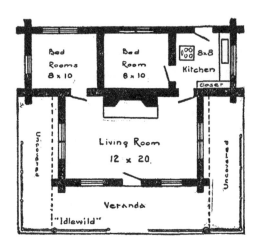

If one of the windows in the end should be of generous size, it would enable you to stow your canoes very conveniently here in the absence of a boathouse.

The Jolly Pines

The Jolly Pines is a compact cabin, with ample room for the full enjoyment of such of the vacation time as must be lived indoors.

The front door of the living room is double and the windows are of the casement type, so that the entire front of the house may practically be thrown open.

In this case the chimney is built up inside the cabin and occupies a corner of the room. The partitions should be carried up to meet the slant of the roof, and thus you will obtain a large and airy room of special interest, because of the varying pitches of the roof, with its system of rafters and the unusual situation of the fireplace. This

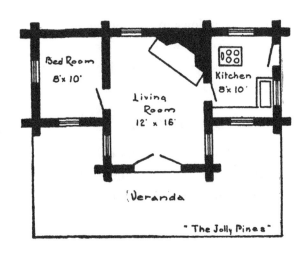

Bed Room
8' x 10'

Living
Room
12' x 16'

Kitchen
8' x 10'

Veranda

"The Jolly Pines"

The Hermitage.

A FEW PLANS

should face the front door as nearly as possible.

The bedroom and kitchen may be floored over to gain additional storage space and to assist in keeping the temperature down.

The Antlers

By partitioning off part of the veranda one gains considerable space, which may be utilized as a bedroom. If more porch room is needed, it may easily be obtained by adding an uncovered veranda to the end of the house.

Should you desire to build the chimney outside the cabin, cut a hole in the wall large enough for the fireplace, including the shelf. Then proceed to build according to the directions in the body of the book. The fireplace need not in this case project very far into the room. A small window on either side of the fireplace and high up would assist materially in obtaining a

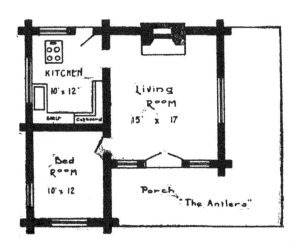

KITCHEN
10' x 12'

SHELF Cupboard

Living
Room
15' x 17'

Bed
Room
10' x 12

Porch
"The Antlers"

"The Antlers"

draught on a hot day. This would leave space beneath for bookshelves, seats, or gun cases, etc. In any of the structures do not fail to make ample allowance for the storage of dishes and supplies. It may often happen that a space beneath the floor reached by a trapdoor could be built with little trouble and large gain.

The size of the kitchen might be curtailed if it seems desirable to make the bedroom larger.

Whenever half doors are used a batten should be placed on the upper half that will lap over the lower half about one inch. This will give you protection from draughts and from the driving rains which often beat against the walls beneath the porch roofs.

155

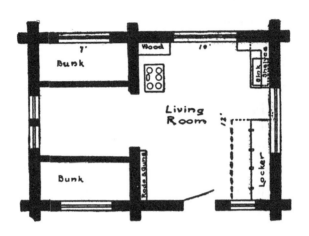

Bunk

Wood

7'

10'

Bunk

Rods & Guns

Living Room

Sink
Shelves

Locker

Sleepy Hollow

A FEW PLANS

Sleepy Hollow

Sleepy Hollow is a cabin that can be kept warm without much expenditure of wood, or it may be thrown open during the warmer periods and thus provides a camp which may be built at little cost and in which one might be perfectly comfortable at any time of year.

Its easy construction recommends it, and a small family should find its simple care and convenience a helpful source of pleasure during the outing season. For the same reason a party of fishermen or hunters will be none the less grateful.

The large windows make the bedroom into practically an outdoor sleeping room. The windows should, of course, be kept rather higher from the floor than in the living room. A curtain may be stretched across the doorway and provision made

157

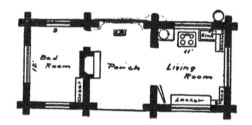

The Hermitage,

for a curtain to divide the bedroom in the event of guests.

The locker in the living room should be made with a false top which may be hinged and thrown over to provide an additional bed in case of an overflow.

The Hermitage

This is another camp of easy construction and calls for few logs of any considerable length. The number of corners involves a little extra notching, but the short length of the logs makes the handling quite simple.

The porch may be provided with screens and screen doors set therein, all of which should be made in sections and may be stored overhead in the bedroom. This provides an outdoor sleeping room, though in regions where mosquitos are plentiful a screen to fit the fireplace open-

159

ing should be made, otherwise they will surely find you out.

By the way, ordinary wire screening is no protection against black flies, mosquitos, etc. It merely provides a multitude of doorways through which they proceed in dignified silence and then plane merrily in your direction, feeling refreshed after the momentary rest. Mosquito bar is the thing, tacked over the wire screening, to be removed as the season advances and the house fly becomes the only undesirable guest.

Should the camp be erected in a hunting country, wooden sections to fit the openings with doors and windows set in can be built, and thus the camp may be enclosed and made warm and comfortable, even in the winter.

160

A FEW PLANS

The Rookery

The Rookery is a small camp, arranged to give an abundance of room and comfort. It can be built without difficulty and the cost may be kept within reasonable limits. On the outside, porches may be added as desired and must present a large and pleasing appearance.

The divisions of the rooms may be made of ordinary lumber, stained, which would be cheaper and more quickly accomplished than by using logs for the partitions, though the latter are much to be preferred if the camp is to maintain its character.

A substitute may be found in peeled slabs which may be obtained at saw mills. These are to be squared on two edges and nailed to 2 x 4 studding, the slabs to run horizontally and the cracks between to be plastered to still further carry out the appearance of the main walls.

161

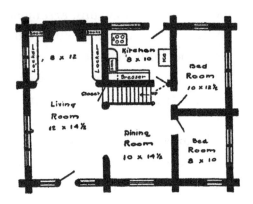

Locker, 8 x 12

Kitchen
8 x 10

Locker

Bed
Room
10 x 12½

Dresser

Closet

Living
Room
12 x 14½

Dining
Room
10 x 14½

Bed
Room
8 x 10

The Rookery

At the doorway, round poles are to be used and faced to take the door and window frames. Round poles are also to be used at the opening to the dining room and ingle nook. These poles, being firmly set, will furnish support for the ends of the short logs making the partitions. The other end of the log may be notched to fit the side wall logs and need not be laid with the side walls as shown in the plan. Spike from the top sides so that the spikes will be hidden.

By careful planning all the small ends of logs may be utilized in the partitions.

The windows in the living room and dining room should be set low, in order that the view from the interior of the rooms may be as complete and pleasing as possible. Under the bookshelves in the ingle nook, wood lockers may be built, bringing them flush with the masonry of the chimney and providing, if desired, doors from the outside to enable one to

163

fill the boxes without going through the rooms.

The floor of the ingle nook might be paved with flat stones laid in cement, to make an extended hearth. This is not a hard task and will repay one for the trouble taken in the character gained in the room.

If the living room is not ceiled overhead, the steps may be reversed to run from this room up to the room above, which will be of good size and may be supplied with beds. If the upper floor is to be used for sleeping, a dormer window of generous size and in harmony with the lines of the building should be built into the roof.

Leaving the living room open to the roof will make this a delightful room indeed, with ample space for the hanging of trophies and a general feeling of largeness and air much to be desired.

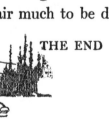

THE END

A CATALOG OF SELECTED
DOVER BOOKS
IN ALL FIELDS OF INTEREST

A CATALOG OF SELECTED DOVER
BOOKS IN ALL FIELDS OF INTEREST

100 BEST-LOVED POEMS, Edited by Philip Smith. *"The Passionate Shepherd to His Love," "Shall I compare thee to a summer's day?" "Death, be not proud," "The Raven," "The Road Not Taken," plus works by Blake, Wordsworth, Byron, Shelley, Keats, many others. Includes 13 selections from the Common Core State Standards Initiative.* 112pp.   0-486-28553-7

1000 TURN-OF-THE-CENTURY HOUSES: With Illustrations and Floor Plans, Herbert C. Chivers. Reproduced from a rare edition, this showcase of homes ranges from cottages and bungalows to sprawling mansions. Each house is meticulously illustrated and accompanied by complete floor plans. 256pp.   0-486-45596-3

101 GREAT AMERICAN POEMS, Edited by The American Poetry & Literacy Project. Rich treasury of verse from the 19th and 20th centuries includes works by Edgar Allan Poe, Robert Frost, Walt Whitman, Langston Hughes, Emily Dickinson, T. S. Eliot, other notables. Includes 13 selections from the Common Core State Standards Initiative. 96pp.   0-486-40158-8

20TH-CENTURY FASHION ILLUSTRATION: The Feminine Ideal, Rosemary Torre. Introduction by Harold Koda. This captivating retrospective explores the social context of fashion with informative text and over 70 striking images. Profiles include flappers, glamour girls, flower children, and the modern obsession with celebrity styles. 176pp.   0-486-46963-8

3200 OLD-TIME CUTS AND ORNAMENTS, Edited by Blanche Cirker. Royalty-free pictures from 1909 French typography catalog: plants, animals, religious motifs, music, carriages, boats, sports, furniture, clothing; plus borders, banners, wreaths, and other ornaments. Over 3,200 black-and-white illustrations. 112pp.   0-486-41732-8

500 YEARS OF ILLUSTRATION: From Albrecht Dürer to Rockwell Kent, Howard Simon. Unrivaled treasury of art from the 1500s through the 1900s includes drawings by Goya, Hogarth, Dürer, Morris, Doré, Beardsley, others. Hundreds of illustrations, brief introductions. Ideal as reference and browsing book. 512pp.   0-486-48465-3

ABC BOOK OF EARLY AMERICANA, Eric Sloane. Artist and historian Eric Sloane presents a wondrous A-to-Z collection of American innovations, including hex signs, ear trumpets, popcorn, and rocking chairs. Illustrated, hand-lettered pages feature brief captions explaining objects' origins and uses. 64pp.   0-486-49808-5

ADVENTURES OF HUCKLEBERRY FINN, Mark Twain. Join Huck and Jim as their boyhood adventures along the Mississippi River lead them into a world of excitement, danger, and self-discovery. Humorous narrative, lyrical descriptions of the Mississippi valley, and memorable characters. 224pp.   0-486-28061-6

ALICE STARMORE'S BOOK OF FAIR ISLE KNITTING, Alice Starmore. A noted designer from the region of Scotland's Fair Isle explores the history and techniques of this distinctive, stranded-color knitting style and provides copious illustrated instructions for 14 original knitwear designs. 208pp.   0-486-47218-3

CATALOG OF DOVER BOOKS

ALICE'S ADVENTURES IN WONDERLAND, Lewis Carroll. Beloved classic about a little girl lost in a topsy-turvy land and her encounters with the White Rabbit, March Hare, Mad Hatter, Cheshire Cat, and other delightfully improbable characters. 42 illustrations by Sir John Tenniel. A selection of the Common Core State Standards Initiative. 96pp. 0-486-27543-4

AMERICAN BALLADS AND FOLK SONGS, John A. Lomax and Alan Lomax. Music and lyrics for over 200 songs. *John Henry, Goin' Home, Little Brown Jug, Alabama-Bound, Black Betty, The Hammer Song, Jesse James, Down in the Valley, The Ballad of Davy Crockett,* and many more. 672pp. 0-486-28276-7

AMERICAN LOCOMOTIVES IN HISTORIC PHOTOGRAPHS: 1858 to 1949, Ron Ziel. A rare collection of 126 meticulously detailed official photographs, called "builder portraits," majestically chronicle the rise of steam locomotive power in America. Introduction. Detailed captions. 140pp. 0-486-27393-8

ANIMALS: 1,419 Copyright-Free Illustrations of Mammals, Birds, Fish, Insects, etc, Selected by Jim Harter. Selected for its visual impact and ease of use, this outstanding collection of wood engravings presents over 1,000 species of animals in extremely lifelike poses. Includes mammals, birds, reptiles, amphibians, fish, insects, and other invertebrates. 284pp. 0-486-23766-4

THE ANNOTATED INNOCENCE OF FATHER BROWN, G. K. Chesterton. Twelve of the popular Father Brown mysteries appear in this copiously annotated edition. Includes "The Blue Cross," "The Hammer of God," "The Eye of Apollo," and more. 352pp. 0-486-29859-0

ANTIGONE, Sophocles. Filled with passionate speeches and sensitive probing of moral and philosophical issues, this powerful and often-performed Greek drama reveals the grim fate that befalls the children of Oedipus. Footnotes. 64pp. 0-486-27804-2

ART FORMS IN NATURE, Ernst Haeckel. Multitude of strangely beautiful natural forms: Radiolaria, Foraminifera, Ciliata, diatoms, calcareous sponges, Tubulariidae, Siphonophora, Semaeostomeae, star corals, starfishes, much more. All images in black and white. 100pp. 0-486-22987-4

THE ART OF WAR, Sun Tzu. Widely regarded as "The Oldest Military Treatise in the World," this landmark work covers principles of strategy, tactics, maneuvering, communication, and supplies; the use of terrain, fire, and the seasons of the year; much more. 96pp. 0-486-42557-6

THE ARTHUR RACKHAM TREASURY: 86 Full-Color Illustrations, Arthur Rackham. Selected and Edited by Jeff A. Menges. A stunning treasury of 86 full-page plates span the famed English artist's career, from *Rip Van Winkle* (1905) to masterworks such as *Undine, A Midsummer Night's Dream,* and *Wind in the Willows* (1939). 96pp. 0-486-44685-9

THE AUTHENTIC GILBERT & SULLIVAN SONGBOOK, W. S. Gilbert and A. S. Sullivan. The most comprehensive collection available, this songbook includes selections from every one of Gilbert and Sullivan's light operas. Ninety-two numbers are presented uncut and unedited, and in their original keys. 410pp. 0-486-23482-7

THE AUTOCRAT OF THE BREAKFAST-TABLE, Oliver Wendell Holmes. Witty, easy-to-read philosophical essays, written by the poet, essayist, and professor. Holmes drew upon his experiences as a resident of a New England boardinghouse to add color and humor to these reflections. 240pp. 0-486-79028-2

THE AWAKENING, Kate Chopin. First published in 1899, this controversial novel of a New Orleans wife's search for love outside a stifling marriage shocked readers. Today, it remains a first-rate narrative with superb characterization. New introductory note. 128pp. 0-486-27786-0

Browse over 10,000 books at www.doverpublications.com

BASEBALL IS . . .: Defining the National Pastime, Edited by Paul Dickson. Wisecracking, philosophical, nostalgic, and entertaining, these hundreds of quips and observations by players, their wives, managers, authors, and others cover every aspect of our national pastime. It's a great any-occasion gift for fans! 256pp.   0-486-48209-X

BEETHOVEN'S LETTERS, Ludwig van Beethoven. Edited by Dr. A. C. Kalischer. Features 457 letters to fellow musicians, friends, greats, patrons, and literary men. Reveals musical thoughts, quirks of personality, insights, and daily events. Includes 15 plates. 410pp.   0-486-22769-3

BOUND & DETERMINED: A Visual History of Corsets, 1850–1960, Kristina Seleshanko. This revealing history of corsetry ranges from the 19th through the mid-20th centuries to show how simple laced bodices developed into corsets of cane, whalebone, and steel. Lavish illustrations include line drawings and photographs. 128pp.   0-486-47892-0

THE BUILDING OF MANHATTAN, Written and Illustrated by Donald A. Mackay. Meticulously accurate line drawings and fascinating text explain construction above and below ground, including excavating subway lines and building bridges and skyscrapers. Hundreds of illustrations reveal intricate details of construction techniques. A selection of the Common Core State Standards Initiative. 160pp.   0-486-47317-1

THE BUNGALOW BOOK: Floor Plans and Photos of 112 Houses, 1910, Henry L. Wilson. Here are 112 of the most popular and economic blueprints of the early 20th century — plus an illustration or photograph of each completed house. A wonderful time capsule that still offers a wealth of valuable insights. 160pp.   0-486-45104-6

THE CALL OF THE WILD, Jack London. A classic novel of adventure, drawn from London's own experiences as a Klondike adventurer, relating the story of a heroic dog caught in the brutal life of the Alaska Gold Rush. Note. 64pp.   0-486-26472-6

CANDIDE, Voltaire. Edited by Francois-Marie Arouet. One of the world's great satires since its first publication in 1759. Witty, caustic skewering of romance, science, philosophy, religion, government — nearly all human ideals and institutions. A selection of the Common Core State Standards Initiative. 112pp.   0-486-26689-3

THE CARTOON HISTORY OF TIME, Kate Charlesworth and John Gribbin. Cartoon characters explain cosmology, quantum physics, and other concepts covered by Stephen Hawking's *A Brief History of Time*. Humorous graphic novel–style treatment, perfect for young readers and curious folk of all ages. 64pp.   0-486-49097-1

THE CHERRY ORCHARD, Anton Chekhov. Classic of world drama concerns passing of semifeudal order in turn-of-the-century Russia, symbolized in the sale of the cherry orchard owned by Madame Ranevskaya. Showcases Chekhov's rich sensitivities as an observer of human nature. 64pp.   0-486-26682-6

A CHRISTMAS CAROL, Charles Dickens. This engrossing tale relates Ebenezer Scrooge's ghostly journeys through Christmases past, present, and future and his ultimate transformation from a harsh and grasping old miser to a charitable and compassionate human being. 80pp.   0-486-26865-9

COMMON SENSE, Thomas Paine. First published in January of 1776, this highly influential landmark document clearly and persuasively argued for American separation from Great Britain and paved the way for the Declaration of Independence. A selection of the Common Core State Standards Initiative. 64pp.   0-486-29602-4

THE COMPLETE SHORT STORIES OF OSCAR WILDE, Oscar Wilde. Complete texts of "The Happy Prince and Other Tales," "A House of Pomegranates," "Lord Arthur Savile's Crime and Other Stories," "Poems in Prose," and "The Portrait of Mr. W. H." 208pp.   0-486-45216-6

COMPLETE SONNETS, William Shakespeare. Over 150 exquisite poems deal with love, friendship, the tyranny of time, beauty's evanescence, death, and other themes in language of remarkable power, precision, and beauty. Glossary of archaic terms. Includes a selection from the Common Core State Standards Initiative. 80pp. 0-486-26686-9

THE COUNT OF MONTE CRISTO: Abridged Edition, Alexandre Dumas. Falsely accused of treason, Edmond Dantès is imprisoned in the bleak Chateau d'If. After a hair-raising escape, he launches an elaborate plot to extract a bitter revenge against those who betrayed him. 448pp. 0-486-45643-9

CRAFTSMAN BUNGALOWS: 59 Homes from "The Craftsman," Edited by Gustav Stickley. Best and most attractive designs from the Arts and Crafts Movement publication from 1903 to 1916 includes sketches, photographs of homes, floor plans, and descriptive text. 128pp. 0-486-25829-7

CRIME AND PUNISHMENT, Fyodor Dostoyevsky. Translated by Constance Garnett. Supreme masterpiece tells the story of Raskolnikov, a student tormented by his own thoughts after he murders an old woman. Overwhelmed by guilt and terror, he confesses and goes to prison. A selection of the Common Core State Standards Initiative. 448pp. 0-486-41587-2

CYRANO DE BERGERAC, Edmond Rostand. A quarrelsome, hot-tempered, and unattractive swordsman falls hopelessly in love with a beautiful woman and woos her for a handsome but slow-witted suitor. A witty and eloquent drama. 144pp. 0-486-41119-2

DANIEL BOONE'S OWN STORY & THE ADVENTURES OF DANIEL BOONE, Daniel Boone and Francis Lister Hawks. This two-part tale features reminiscences in the legendary frontiersman's own words and a profile of his entire life, with exciting accounts of blazing the Wilderness Road and serving as a militiaman during the Revolutionary War. 128pp. 0-486-47690-1

THE DECLARATION OF INDEPENDENCE AND OTHER GREAT DOCUMENTS OF AMERICAN HISTORY: 1775-1865, Edited by John Grafton. Thirteen compelling and influential documents: Henry's "Give Me Liberty or Give Me Death," Declaration of Independence, The Constitution, Washington's First Inaugural Address, The Monroe Doctrine, The Emancipation Proclamation, Gettysburg Address, more. Includes 3 selections from the Common Core State Standards Initiative. 64pp. 0-486-41124-9

A DOLL'S HOUSE, Henrik Ibsen. Ibsen's best-known play displays his genius for realistic prose drama. An expression of women's rights, the play climaxes when the central character, Nora, rejects a smothering marriage and life in "a doll's house." A selection of the Common Core State Standards Initiative. 80pp. 0-486-27062-9

DOOMED SHIPS: Great Ocean Liner Disasters, William H. Miller, Jr. Nearly 200 photographs, many from private collections, highlight tales of some of the vessels whose pleasure cruises ended in catastrophe: the *Morro Castle, Normandie, Andrea Doria, Europa,* and many others. 128pp. 0-486-45366-9

THE DORÉ BIBLE ILLUSTRATIONS, Gustave Doré. Detailed plates from the Bible: the Creation scenes, Adam and Eve, horrifying visions of the Flood, the battle sequences with their monumental crowds, depictions of the life of Jesus, 241 plates in all. 241pp. 0-486-23004-X

DUBLINERS, James Joyce. A fine and accessible introduction to the work of one of the 20th century's most influential writers, this collection features 15 tales, including a masterpiece of the short-story genre, "The Dead." 160pp. 0-486-26870-5

THE EARLY SCIENCE FICTION OF PHILIP K. DICK, Philip K. Dick. This anthology presents short stories and novellas that originally appeared in pulp magazines of the early 1950s, including "The Variable Man," "Second Variety," "Beyond the Door," "The Defenders," and more. 272pp. 0-486-49733-X

Browse over 10,000 books at www.doverpublications.com

THE EARLY SHORT STORIES OF F. SCOTT FITZGERALD, F. Scott Fitzgerald. These tales offer insights into many themes, characters, and techniques that emerged in Fitzgerald's later works. Selections include "The Curious Case of Benjamin Button," "Babes in the Woods," and a dozen others. 256pp. 0-486-79465-2

EASY BUTTERFLY ORIGAMI, Tammy Yee. Thirty full-color designs to fold include simple instructions and fun facts about each species. Patterns are perforated for easy removal and offer accurate portrayals of variations in insects' top and bottom sides. 64pp. 0-486-78457-6

EASY SPANISH PHRASE BOOK NEW EDITION: Over 700 Phrases for Everyday Use, Pablo Garcia Loaeza, Ph.D. Up-to-date volume, organized for quick access to phrases related to greetings, transportation, shopping, emergencies, other common circumstances. Over 700 entries include terms for modern telecommunications, idioms, slang. Phonetic pronunciations accompany phrases. 96pp. 0-486-49905-7

EINSTEIN'S ESSAYS IN SCIENCE, Albert Einstein. Speeches and essays in accessible, everyday language profile influential physicists such as Niels Bohr and Isaac Newton. They also explore areas of physics to which the author made major contributions. 128pp. 0-486-47011-3

EL DORADO: Further Adventures of the Scarlet Pimpernel, Baroness Orczy. A popular sequel to *The Scarlet Pimpernel*, this suspenseful story recounts the Pimpernel's attempts to rescue the Dauphin from imprisonment during the French Revolution. An irresistible blend of intrigue, period detail, and vibrant characterizations. 352pp. 0-486-44026-5

ELEGANT SMALL HOMES OF THE TWENTIES: 99 Designs from a Competition, Chicago Tribune. Nearly 100 designs for five- and six-room houses feature New England and Southern colonials, Normandy cottages, stately Italianate dwellings, and other fascinating snapshots of American domestic architecture of the 1920s. 112pp. 0-486-46910-7

THE ELUSIVE PIMPERNEL, Baroness Orczy. Robespierre's revolutionaries find their wicked schemes thwarted by the heroic Pimpernel — Sir Percival Blakeney. In this thrilling sequel, Chauvelin devises a plot to eliminate the Pimpernel and his wife. 272pp. 0-486-45464-9

ERIC SLOANE'S WEATHER BOOK, Eric Sloane. A beautifully illustrated book of enlightening lore for outdoorsmen, farmers, sailors, and anyone who has ever wondered whether to take an umbrella when leaving the house. 87 illustrations. 96pp. 0-486-44357-4

ETHAN FROME, Edith Wharton. Classic story of wasted lives, set against a bleak New England background. Superbly delineated characters in a hauntingly grim tale of thwarted love. Considered by many to be Wharton's masterpiece. 96pp. 0-486-26690-7

THE FEDERALIST PAPERS, Alexander Hamilton, James Madison, John Jay. A collection of 85 articles and essays that were initially published anonymously in New York newspapers in 1787–1788, this volume reflects the intentions of the Constitution's framers and ratifiers. 448pp. 0-486-49636-8

FINDING YOUR WAY WITHOUT MAP OR COMPASS, Harold Gatty. Useful, instructive manual shows would-be explorers, hikers, bikers, scouts, sailors, and survivalists how to find their way outdoors by observing animals, weather patterns, shifting sands, and other elements of nature. 288pp. 0-486-40613-X

FIRST SPANISH READER: A Beginner's Dual-Language Book, Edited by Angel Flores. Delightful stories, other material based on works of Don Juan Manuel, Luis Taboada, Ricardo Palma, other noted writers. Complete faithful English translations on facing pages. Exercises. 176pp. 0-486-25810-6

Browse over 10,000 books at www.doverpublications.com

CATALOG OF DOVER BOOKS

FIVE ACRES AND INDEPENDENCE, M. G. Kains. This classic of the back-to-the-land movement is packed with solid, timeless information. Written by a renowned horticulturist, it has taught generations how to make their land self-sufficient. 95 figures. 397pp. 0-486-20974-1

FLATLAND: A Romance of Many Dimensions, Edwin A. Abbott. Classic of science (and mathematical) fiction — charmingly illustrated by the author — describes the adventures of A. Square, a resident of Flatland, in Spaceland (three dimensions), Lineland (one dimension), and Pointland (no dimensions). 96pp. 0-486-27263-X

FRANKENSTEIN, Mary Shelley. The story of Victor Frankenstein's monstrous creation and the havoc it caused has enthralled generations of readers and inspired countless writers of horror and suspense. With the author's own 1831 introduction. 176pp. 0-486-28211-2

THE GARGOYLE BOOK: 572 Examples from Gothic Architecture, Lester Burbank Bridaham. Dispelling the conventional wisdom that French Gothic architectural flourishes were born of despair or gloom, Bridaham reveals the whimsical nature of these creations and the ingenious artisans who made them. 572 illustrations. 224pp. 0-486-44754-5

THE GIFT OF THE MAGI AND OTHER SHORT STORIES, O. Henry. Sixteen captivating stories by one of America's most popular storytellers. Included are such classics as "The Gift of the Magi," "The Last Leaf," and "The Ransom of Red Chief." Publisher's Note. A selection of the Common Core State Standards Initiative. 96pp. 0-486-27061-0

THE GÖDELIAN PUZZLE BOOK: Puzzles, Paradoxes and Proofs, Raymond M. Smullyan. These logic puzzles provide entertaining variations on Gödel's incompleteness theorems, offering ingenious challenges related to infinity, truth and provability, undecidability, and other concepts. No background in formal logic is necessary. 288pp. 0-486-49705-4

THE GOETHE TREASURY: Selected Prose and Poetry, Johann Wolfgang von Goethe. Edited, Selected, and with an Introduction by Thomas Mann. In addition to his lyric poetry, Goethe wrote travel sketches, autobiographical studies, essays, letters, and proverbs in rhyme and prose. This collection presents outstanding examples from each genre. 368pp. 0-486-44780-4

GREAT EXPECTATIONS, Charles Dickens. Orphaned Pip is apprenticed to the dirty work of the forge but dreams of becoming a gentleman — and one day finds himself in possession of "great expectations." Dickens' finest novel. 384pp. 0-486-41586-4

GREAT ILLUSTRATIONS BY N. C. WYETH, N. C. Wyeth. Edited and with an Introduction by Jeff A. Menges. This full-color collection focuses on the artist's early and most popular illustrations, featuring more than 100 images from The Mysterious Stranger, Robin Hood, Robinson Crusoe, The Boy's King Arthur, and other classics. 128pp. 0-486-47295-7

HAMLET, William Shakespeare. The quintessential Shakespearean tragedy, whose highly charged confrontations and anguished soliloquies probe depths of human feeling rarely sounded in any art. Reprinted from an authoritative British edition complete with illuminating footnotes. A selection of the Common Core State Standards Initiative. 128pp. 0-486-27278-8

THE HAUNTED HOUSE, Charles Dickens. A Yuletide gathering in an eerie country retreat provides the backdrop for Dickens and his friends — including Elizabeth Gaskell and Wilkie Collins — who take turns spinning supernatural yarns. 144pp. 0-486-46309-5

THE HEADS OF CERBERUS, Francis Stevens. Illustrated by Ric Binkley. A trio of time-travelers land in Philadelphia's brutal totalitarian state of 2118. Loaded with action and humor, this 1919 classic was the first alternate-world fantasy. "A much-sought rarity." — Analog. 192pp. 0-486-79026-6

Browse over 10,000 books at www.doverpublications.com

CATALOG OF DOVER BOOKS

HEART OF DARKNESS, Joseph Conrad. Dark allegory of a journey up the Congo River and the narrator's encounter with the mysterious Mr. Kurtz. Masterly blend of adventure, character study, psychological penetration. For many, Conrad's finest, most enigmatic story. 80pp. 0-486-26464-5

HISTORIC COSTUMES AND HOW TO MAKE THEM, Mary Fernald and E. Shenton. Practical, informative guidebook shows how to create everything from short tunics worn by Saxon men in the fifth century to a lady's bustle dress of the late 1800s. 81 illustrations. 176pp. 0-486-44906-8

THE HOUND OF THE BASKERVILLES, Sir Arthur Conan Doyle. A deadly curse in the form of a legendary ferocious beast continues to claim its victims from the Baskerville family until Holmes and Watson intervene. Often called the best detective story ever written. 128pp. 0-486-28214-7

THE HOUSE BEHIND THE CEDARS, Charles W. Chesnutt. Originally published in 1900, this groundbreaking novel by a distinguished African-American author recounts the drama of a brother and sister who "pass for white" during the dangerous days of Reconstruction. 208pp. 0-186-46144-0

HOW THE OTHER HALF LIVES, Jacob Riis. This famous journalistic record of the filth and degradation of New York's slums at the turn of the 20th century is a classic in social thought and of early American photography. Over 100 photographs. 256pp. 0-486-22012-5

HOW TO DRAW NEARLY EVERYTHING, Victor Perard. Beginners of all ages can learn to draw figures, faces, landscapes, trees, flowers, and animals of all kinds. Well-illustrated guide offers suggestions for pencil, pen, and brush techniques plus composition, shading, and perspective. 160pp. 0-486-49848-4

HOW TO MAKE SUPER POP-UPS, Joan Irvine. Illustrated by Linda Hendry. Super pop-ups extend the element of surprise with three-dimensional designs that slide, turn, spring, and snap. More than 30 patterns and 475 illustrations include cards, stage props, and school projects. 96pp. 0-486-46589-6

THE IMITATION OF CHRIST, Thomas à Kempis. Translated by Aloysius Croft and Harold Bolton. This religious classic has brought understanding and comfort to millions for centuries. Written in a candid and conversational style, the topics include liberation from worldly inclinations, preparation and consolations of prayer, and eucharistic communion. 160pp. 0-486-43185-1

THE IMPORTANCE OF BEING EARNEST, Oscar Wilde. Wilde's witty and buoyant comedy of manners, filled with some of literature's most famous epigrams, reprinted from an authoritative British edition. Considered Wilde's most perfect work. A selection of the Common Core State Standards Initiative. 64pp. 0-486-26478-5

THE INFERNO, Dante Alighieri. Translated and with notes by Henry Wadsworth Longfellow. The first stop on Dante's famous journey from Hell to Purgatory to Paradise, this 14th-century allegorical poem blends vivid and shocking imagery with graceful lyricism. Translated by the beloved 19th-century poet, Henry Wadsworth Longfellow. 256pp. 0-486-44288-8

JANE EYRE, Charlotte Brontë. Written in 1847, *Jane Eyre* tells the tale of an orphan girl's progress from the custody of cruel relatives to an oppressive boarding school and its culmination in a troubled career as a governess. A selection of the Common Core State Standards Initiative. 448pp. 0-486-42449-9

JAPANESE WOODBLOCK BIRD PRINTS, Numata Kashû. These lifelike images of birds and flowers first appeared in a now-rare 1883 portfolio. A magnificent reproduction of a 1938 facsimile of the original publication, this exquisite edition features 150 color illustrations. 160pp. 0-486-47050-4

Browse over 10,000 books at www.doverpublications.com

JULIUS CAESAR, William Shakespeare. Great tragedy based on Plutarch's account of the lives of Brutus, Julius Caesar, and Mark Antony. Evil plotting, ringing oratory, high tragedy with Shakespeare's incomparable insight, dramatic power. Explanatory footnotes. 96pp. 0-486-26876-4

THE JUNGLE, Upton Sinclair. 1906 bestseller shockingly reveals intolerable labor practices and working conditions in the Chicago stockyards as it tells the grim story of a Slavic family that emigrates to America full of optimism but soon faces despair. 304pp. 0-486-41923-1

JUST WHAT THE DOCTOR DISORDERED: Early Writings and Cartoons of Dr. Seuss, Dr. Seuss. Edited and with an Introduction by Rick Marschall. The Doctor's visual hilarity, nonsense language, and offbeat sense of humor illuminate this compilation of items from his early career, created for periodicals such as *Judge, Life, College Humor,* and *Liberty.* 144pp. 0-486-49846-8

KING LEAR, William Shakespeare. Powerful tragedy of an aging king, betrayed by his daughters, robbed of his kingdom, descending into madness. Perhaps the bleakest of Shakespeare's tragic dramas, complete with explanatory footnotes. 144pp. 0-486-28058-6

KNITTING FOR ANARCHISTS: The What, Why and How of Knitting, Anna Zilboorg. Every knitter takes a different approach, and this revolutionary guide encourages experimentation and self-expression. Suitable for active knitters and beginners alike, it offers illustrated patterns for sweaters, pullovers, and cardigans. 160pp. 0-486-79466-0

THE LADY OR THE TIGER?: and Other Logic Puzzles, Raymond M. Smullyan. Created by a renowned puzzle master, these whimsically themed challenges involve paradoxes about probability, time, and change; metapuzzles; and self-referentiality. Nineteen chapters advance in difficulty from relatively simple to highly complex. 1982 edition. 240pp. 0-486-47027-X

LEAVES OF GRASS: The Original 1855 Edition, Walt Whitman. Whitman's immortal collection includes some of the greatest poems of modern times, including his masterpiece, "Song of Myself." Shattering standard conventions, it stands as an unabashed celebration of body and nature. 128pp. 0-486-45676-5

LES MISÉRABLES, Victor Hugo. Translated by Charles E. Wilbour. Abridged by James K. Robinson. A convict's heroic struggle for justice and redemption plays out against a fiery backdrop of the Napoleonic wars. This edition features the excellent original translation and a sensitive abridgment. 304pp. 0-486-45789-3

LIGHT FOR THE ARTIST, Ted Seth Jacobs. Intermediate and advanced art students receive a broad vocabulary of effects with this in-depth study of light. Diagrams and paintings illustrate applications of principles to figure, still life, and landscape paintings. 144pp. 0-486-49304-0

LILITH: A Romance, George MacDonald. In this novel by the father of fantasy literature, a man travels through time to meet Adam and Eve and to explore humanity's fall from grace and ultimate redemption. 240pp. 0-486-46818-6

LINE: An Art Study, Edmund J. Sullivan. Written by a noted artist and teacher, this well-illustrated guide introduces the basics of line drawing. Topics include third and fourth dimensions, formal perspective, shade and shadow, figure drawing, and other essentials. 208pp. 0-486-79484-9

THE LODGER, Marie Belloc Lowndes. Acclaimed by *The New York Times* as "one of the best suspense novels ever written," this novel recounts an English couple's doubts about their boarder, whom they suspect of being a serial killer. 240pp. 0-486-78809-1

"THE LOVELIEST HOME THAT EVER WAS": The Story of the Mark Twain House in Hartford, Steve Courtney. With an Introduction by Hal Holbrook. The official guide to The Mark Twain House & Museum, this volume tells the dramatic story of the author and his family and their Victorian mansion. Architectural drawings, period photos, plus modern color images. 144pp. 0-486-48634-6

MACBETH, William Shakespeare. A Scottish nobleman murders the king in order to succeed to the throne. Tortured by his conscience and fearful of discovery, he becomes tangled in a web of treachery and deceit that ultimately spells his doom. A selection of the Common Core State Standards Initiative. 96pp. 0-486-27802-6

MANHATTAN IN MAPS 1527–2014, Paul E. Cohen and Robert T. Augustyn. This handsome volume features 65 full-color maps charting Manhattan's development from the first Dutch settlement to the present. Each map is placed in context by an accompanying essay. 176pp. 0-486-77991-2

MANHATTAN MOVES UPTOWN: An Illustrated History, Charles Lockwood. Compiled from newspaper archives and richly illustrated with historic images, this fascinating chronicle traces the city's growth from Wall Street to Harlem during the period between 1783 and the early 20th century. 368pp. 0-486-78120-8

MATHEMATICS FOR THE NONMATHEMATICIAN, Morris Kline. Erudite and entertaining overview follows development of mathematics from ancient Greeks to present. Topics include logic and mathematics, the fundamental concept, differential calculus, probability theory, much more. Exercises and problems. 672pp. 0-486-24823-2

MEDEA, Euripides. One of the most powerful and enduring of Greek tragedies, masterfully portraying the fierce motives driving Medea's pursuit of vengeance for her husband's insult and betrayal. Authoritative Rex Warner translation. 64pp. 0-486-27548-5

THE MERCHANT BANKERS, Joseph Wechsberg. With a new Foreword by Christopher Kobrak. Fascinating chronicle of the world's great financial families profiles the personalities behind seven legendary banking houses: Hambros, Barings, the Rothschilds, the Warburgs, Deutsche Bank, Lehman Brothers, and Banca Commerciale Italiana. 384pp. 0-486-78118-6

THE METAMORPHOSIS AND OTHER STORIES, Franz Kafka. Excellent new English translations of title story (considered by many critics Kafka's most perfect work), plus "The Judgment," "In the Penal Colony," "A Country Doctor," and "A Report to an Academy." A selection of the Common Core State Standards Initiative. 96pp. 0-486-29030-1

METROPOLIS, Thea von Harbou. This Weimar-era novel of a futuristic society, written by the screenwriter for the iconic 1927 film, was hailed by noted science-fiction authority Forrest J. Ackerman as "a work of genius." 224pp. 0-486-79567-5

MICHAEL PEARSON'S TRADITIONAL KNITTING: Aran, Fair Isle and Fisher Ganseys, New & Expanded Edition, Michael Pearson. This extensive record of unique patterns from the remote fishing villages of Scotland and England combines a social history of the regions with detailed patterns and practical instructions for knitters. Includes new pattern charts and knitting instructions. 264pp. 0-486-46053-3

A MIDSUMMER NIGHT'S DREAM, William Shakespeare. Among the most popular of Shakespeare's comedies, this enchanting play humorously celebrates the vagaries of love as it focuses upon the intertwined romances of several pairs of lovers. Explanatory footnotes. 80pp. 0-486-27067-X

MODULAR CROCHET: The Revolutionary Method for Creating Custom-Designed Pullovers, Judith Copeland. This guide ranks among the most revolutionary and revered books on freeform and improvisational crochet. Even beginners can use its innovative but simple method to make perfect-fit pullovers, turtlenecks, vests, and other garments. 192pp. 0-486-79687-6

Browse over 10,000 books at www.doverpublications.com

THE MONEY CHANGERS, Upton Sinclair. Originally published in 1908, this cautionary novel from the author of *The Jungle* explores corruption within the American system as a group of power brokers joins forces for personal gain, triggering a crash on Wall Street. 192pp. 0-486-46917-4

THE MOST POPULAR HOMES OF THE TWENTIES, William A. Radford. With a New Introduction by Daniel D. Reiff. Based on a rare 1925 catalog, this architectural showcase features floor plans, construction details, and photos of 26 homes, plus articles on entrances, porches, garages, and more. 250 illustrations, 21 color plates. 176pp. 0-486-47028-8

THE MYSTERIOUS MICKEY FINN, Elliot Paul. A multimillionaire's disappearance incites a maelstrom of kidnapping, murder, and a plot to restore the French monarchy. "One of the funniest books we've read in a long time." — *The New York Times.* 256pp. 0-486-24751-1

MYSTICISM: A Study in the Nature and Development of Spiritual Consciousness, Evelyn Underhill. Classic introduction to mysticism and mystical consciousness: awakening of the self, purification, voices and visions, ecstasy and rapture, dark night of the soul, much more. 544pp. 0-486-42238-0

NARRATIVE OF THE LIFE OF FREDERICK DOUGLASS, Frederick Douglass. The impassioned abolitionist and eloquent orator provides graphic descriptions of his childhood and horrifying experiences as a slave as well as a harrowing record of his dramatic escape to the North and eventual freedom. A selection of the Common Core State Standards Initiative. 96pp. 0-486-28499-9

NEW YORK'S FABULOUS LUXURY APARTMENTS: with Original Floor Plans from the Dakota, River House, Olympic Tower and Other Great Buildings, Andrew Alpern. Magnificently illustrated directory of 73 of Manhattan's most splendid addresses includes mini-histories of each building, noting the architect, builder, date of construction, and more. 221 photographs and drawings. 176pp. 0-486-25318-X

THE NIGHT OF THE LONG KNIVES, Fritz Leiber. Deathland's residents are consumed by the urge to murder each other, making partnership of any sort a lethal risk. Novel-length magazine story from the Cold War era by an influential science-fiction author. 112pp. 0-486-79801-1

NUTS & BOLTS: Industrial Jewelry in the Steampunk Style, Marthe Le Van. Use tubes, rods, metal sheets, and other industrial items to create chic jewelry. Detailed instructions for 24 projects feature illustrated step-by-step directions for assembling earrings, necklaces, pins, and other ornaments. 128pp. 0-486-79027-4

OBELISTS FLY HIGH, C. Daly King. Masterpiece of detective fiction portrays murder aboard a 1935 transcontinental flight. Combining an intricate plot and "locked room" scenario, the mystery was praised by *The New York Times* as "a very thrilling story." 288pp. 0-486-25036-9

THE ODYSSEY, Homer. Excellent prose translation of ancient epic recounts adventures of the homeward-bound Odysseus. Fantastic cast of gods, giants, cannibals, sirens, other supernatural creatures — true classic of Western literature. A selection of the Common Core State Standards Initiative. 256pp. 0-486-40654-7

OEDIPUS REX, Sophocles. Landmark of Western drama concerns the catastrophe that ensues when King Oedipus discovers he has inadvertently killed his father and married his mother. Masterly construction, dramatic irony. A selection of the Common Core State Standards Initiative. 64pp. 0-486-26877-2

ONE OF OURS, Willa Cather. The Pulitzer Prize–winning novel about a young Nebraskan looking for something to believe in. Alienated from his parents, rejected by his wife, he finds his destiny on the bloody battlefields of World War I. 352pp. 0-486-45599-8

VILLETTE, Charlotte Brontë. Acclaimed by Virginia Woolf as "Brontë's finest novel," this moving psychological study features a remarkably modern heroine who abandons her native England for a new life as a schoolteacher in Belgium. 480pp. 0-486-45557-2

VOYAGE OF THE BEAGLE, Charles Darwin. Classic of adventure travel and cornerstone in the development of evolutionary theory recounts Darwin's five-year sojourn in South America, where he made the observations that led to his concept of natural selection. 528pp. 0-486-42489-8

WALDEN; OR, LIFE IN THE WOODS, Henry David Thoreau. Accounts of Thoreau's daily life on the shores of Walden Pond outside Concord, Massachusetts, are interwoven with musings on the virtues of self-reliance and individual freedom, on society, government, and other topics. A selection of the Common Core State Standards Initiative. 224pp. 0-486-28495-6

WATERCOLOR, John Pike. From one of America's most popular artists comes information on everything from advice on choosing a brush to producing a variety of washes, brush strokes, and textures. 166 illustrations. 224pp. 0-486-44783-9

WHAT EINSTEIN DIDN'T KNOW: Scientific Answers to Everyday Questions, Robert L. Wolke. From simple (How do magnets work?) to complex (Where does uranium get its energy?), this volume offers intriguing insights into scientific facts. Definitive accounts of workings behind everyday phenomena include related do-it-yourself experiments. 240pp. 0-486-49289-3

WHERE NO MAN HAS GONE BEFORE: A History of NASA's Apollo Lunar Expeditions, William David Compton. Introduction by Paul Dickson. This official NASA history traces behind-the-scenes conflicts and cooperation between scientists and engineers. The first half concerns preparations for the Moon landings, and the second half documents the flights that followed *Apollo 11*. 1989 edition. 432pp. 0-486-47888-2

WORLD WAR II: THE ENCYCLOPEDIA OF THE WAR YEARS, 1941-1945, Norman Polmar and Thomas B. Allen. Authoritative and comprehensive, this reference surveys World War II from an American perspective. Over 2,400 entries cover battles, weapons, and participants as well as aspects of politics, culture, and everyday life. 85 illustrations. 960pp. 0-486-47962-5

WUTHERING HEIGHTS, Emily Brontë. Somber tale of consuming passions and vengeance — played out amid the lonely English moors — recounts the turbulent and tempestuous love story of Cathy and Heathcliff. Poignant and compelling. 256pp. 0-486-29256-8